Of all the leadership books I have read, Co_____ masterful job of piecing together stories of th_____ lessons on how great leadership is directly re_____ anyone in education, and a MUST-READ for _____

Principal
Johnsburg High School
2013 Illinois Principal Association President

Paul Pryma gets under the hood and inside the minds of three of Chicago's greatest basketball coaches. **Coaches of Chicago** *provides a fascinating look at everything that goes into coaching and the incredible drive and intelligence it takes to succeed in the ultra-competitive world of Chicago hoops.*

~Michael O'Brien
Chicago Sun Times

WOW! Like listening to Springsteen! **Coaches of Chicago** *is a treasure box of wisdom for any teacher/ coach who still loves to learn. It is such a joy to read, but more than that it is exactly what a professional development seminar should be. I'm in my sixth decade as a teacher and a coach ("one and the same" to quote the book) and this book reinforced my passion for both. Thanks, Paul.*

~Tom McKenna
Teacher/Coach
St. Ignatius College Prep and Hinsdale Central High School

This uplifting book explores the principles of leadership as only Paul Pryma, educator and coach, could write, masterfully synthesizing the wisdom of world-renown leaders while respectfully uncovering the philosophies and motivations of three prominent coaches from the Chicagoland area. Leaders, no matter what field, will be taken on a journey through the canon of standards for achieving true leadership qualities; coaches will gain an insider's insight into the basketball arena rarely, if ever, revealed; and fans everywhere will fall in love with the game again—for, as Pryma believes, when basketball is coached and played properly, the essence of life suddenly appears as clearly as a well-executed fast-break. Dr. Pryma's passion for leading, educating, and coaching resonates in his writing and will have you reading on the edge of your seat wishing for overtime.

~Richard Kolimas
English Dept. Chair/Coach
Lincoln-Way East High School

I can tell you for a fact that outside of my mother, no one had a more positive influence on my life than the coaches I had in high school. They taught me the importance of hard work, dedication, and the value of integrity. **Coaches of Chicago** *is a must-read for school administrators, coaches, and parents who want to better understand this unique classroom and how coaches help young people become better citizens.*

~Marty Hickman, EdD
Executive Director
Illinois High School Association

Coach Pryma has masterfully synthesized the unique characteristics and traits that great high school coaches employ as leaders. This journey inside Chicago basketball is an educational venture for coaches, educators, and any leaders entrusted with the well-being of young people. Pryma's rich story telling gives life to the virtues of these accomplished coaches.

~Dr. John Planek
NCAA and IHSA Athletic Director

Coaches of Chicago *is not about Chicago…and it is not about coaches, or even basketball. As a leader in corporate America for over twenty-five years, I've had the incredible good fortune to work with, and for, many very successful business leaders. But, the most inspiring leader I've ever worked for is Paul Pryma.* **Coaches of Chicago** *illustrates how even the most inspirational leaders have been inspired by others.*

~Todd Gierke
CFO Curran Group

In *Coaches of Chicago*, Paul Pryma thoughtfully captures the essence of great coaches and great leaders. He provides valuable insights into the makings of teamwork, integrity, and excellence that inspire us to live by our highest values and move beyond our limitations. Through a profile of three local coaching legends, we see the profound effect coaching can have on individuals and organizations in creating success on the court and in life.

~Dr. Barry Rodgers
Principal
Lake Forest High School

Coaches of Chicago is a must-read for anyone in a leadership role. The book inspired me to reflect on my own leadership techniques and how I can improve as a coach. The stories are captivating and written with great detail. This is a great book for all coaches regardless of their sport.

~David Weber
Teacher/Coach
Glenbrook North High School

This book is a must read for not only current coaches and those who aspire to take on one of life's most rewarding challenges but for anyone who wants to be a better leader. Paul Pryma captures the keys to achieving success from some of the best mentors the coaching world has ever had.

~David Kaplan
Television/Radio Host
Comcast, The Game, and WGN

Just as Carl Sandburg's "Chicago Poems" (1916) introduced a plain speaking style to the nation, Paul Pryma's *Coaches of Chicago* succinctly defies the top-down, data-driven test score assessment mania plaguing our nation's schools. Dr. Pryma's analysis of three successful Chicago high school coaches sends many powerful messages to a wide audience of readers spanning fledgeling teacher/coaches to experienced educational leaders. Pryma leads us on a journey of real-life experiences marked by stormy passion, fierce dedication, proud planning, and husky defiance as he shares the life lessons of three coaches who have demonstrated throughout their careers that wrapping your arms around the hearts and minds of youngsters is a pedagogy that must never be forsaken.

~Karl Costello
Athletic Director
Niles North High School

Coaches of Chicago is a must-read for any coach or business executive. I can't imagine a business leader that wouldn't learn from the leadership techniques utilized by the coaches of Chicago and applying it to their own organizations.

~David Brenner
Founding Partner
Paragon Marketing Group, LLC

The story telling is exquisite. I read the book over the course of a week and felt like I was with Paul the entire time. His voice comes through so strongly, it's as if he's sitting in the room with you. Any educator, rookie, or veteran, will walk away from the experience with new insights into the world of teaching and coaching.

~Bryan Halpern
Educator
Glenbrook North High School

Coaches of Chicago is an absolute must-read for all coaches, teachers and leaders across the country. Dr. Pryma a master coach himself pulls back the curtain with this "unusual type of sharing" from three of Chicagoland's basketball coaching legends and the experiences that shaped their coaching and teaching careers. This is a tremendous document that should be required reading for coaches and leaders of all sports. It has changed how I think about coaching, teaching, and being a father. A must-read!

~Tom Livatino
Basketball Coach/Teacher
Loyola Academy

Coaching, teaching, and leading; bundled together it's a recipe for helping people to grow and effectively manage life's daily challenges. Paul Pryma has captured the essence of these in his book. But this is no surprise to anyone who knows Paul. A man with a true moral and educational compass and someone whose core values serve as a benchmark shares all this through his stories and lessons about life. I urge you to read this writing as it is a compilation of serious, funny and heartfelt 'teachable moments.' Reflection is a key to growth and this book truly makes you think with your mind, heart and soul.

~Jim Bloch
Retired Athletic Director
New Trier and Glenbrook North High Schools
Speaker & Consultant
The TEAM Speaking Group

Paul Pryma has hit a clutch three-pointer with his inspiring book about three consummate educators/ basketball coaches. Paul is more than the principal at Glenbrook North High School and a former Wildkits boys' basketball coach at Evanston Township High School; he is also a fervent fan of life changers, aka dedicated coaches at the prep level. His observations of the impact Rick Malnati, Gene Pingatore, and the late Steve Pappas had and continue to have on impressionable teens will move the hoops junkies and casual fans alike. Find out what Pingatore asked future NBA star Isiah Thomas to do to keep St. Joseph Chargers teams focused and motivated; how urgency and honesty fueled Malnati's New Trier teams; and why Pappas never hesitated to tout the value of a custodial staff member to his English class students at Deerfield High School. Particularly poignant throughout the book is the voice of Pappas' widow, Cathie. Her recollections of Steve are detailed and heartwarming, from the day she asked him to teach her basketball skills to the nights he stood beside her, looked up at the stars and asked, "Well, what do you see?" What I took away from this book: Hoops coaches often shine brightly when basketball is the furthest thing from their minds.

~Bill McLean
Senior Writer/Associate Editor
The North Shore Weekend

Pryma's vivid prose reveals the heart of three exceptional coaches who each approached their life's work with the same mantra in mind: educate the whole child. For teachers who share the same purpose and values, this book provides both inspiration and confirmation for re-dedicating themselves to the ideas that perhaps brought them into education in the first place and that the best schools must recognize as central to meeting today's challenges in education.

~Lorena Huguelet
Educator/Journalist

Coaches of Chicago reinforces that Paul Pryma is a man for others. Paul's work has done two great things: 1) He has honored three coaching legends in Illinois, all of whom are very deserving of this recognition; 2) Just as important, Paul has put together a useful tool for any coach, at any level, to learn from. The stories and lessons in this book can help us all improve our craft.

~Paul Harris
Teacher/Coach
Highland Park High School

Written in a unique style, it's a must-read for any coach, teacher, and leader. It's a blend of storytelling and insight but one that highlights various tools to elevate anyone's leadership qualities and, as a result, success through the eyes and actions of three distinguished coaches.

~Joe Henricksen
City/Suburban Hoops Report

Through his own experiences as an outstanding high school principal and basketball coach, Pryma offers practical advice on how to become a better leader. He believes laughter is truly the best medicine for handling the day-to-day challenges that confront school people. It is a lively and highly readable book.

~Dr. Joe Schmidt, AFSC, EdD
President
Saint Patrick High School

COACHES OF CHICAGO

COACHES OF CHICAGO
Inspiring Stories about Leadership and Life

WINDY CITY PUBLISHERS
2118 Plum Grove Road #349
Rolling Meadows, IL 60008
www.windycitypublishers.com

Published in the United States of America

Library of Congress Control Number:
2014949576

ISBN:
978-1-941478-06-6

Back Cover Skyline Photo by Jim Quinn

WINDY CITY PUBLISHERS
CHICAGO

COACHES OF CHICAGO

Inspiring Stories about Leadership and Life

PAUL M. PRYMA

PREFACE

———————————————————●———————————————————

Some of the most transformational education occurs after the regular school day at or about 3 p.m. In gyms and playing fields across America, students are engaged in relevant and project-based learning that helps them to think critically, solve problems, examine justice and ethics, and respect the lessons inspired by failing and succeeding within a collaborative learning environment. The three educators selected for this study, Rick Malnati, Gene Pingatore, and Steve Pappas profoundly influenced the lives of their grateful students and reflect best practice in educational leadership. Successful prep basketball programs in Chicago, Illinois are led by hard working, inspiring, and creative organizers who listen and respond to the individual differences of their students while modeling kindness, resilience, and integrity in a milieu fraught with controversy, scandal, and greed. This book relies upon narrative and interview-based methodology to mine rich stories that chronicle the powerful careers of three legendary Chicago coaches.

The findings of this study revealed four themes of educational leadership: work ethic, keen observation and listening skills, resilience, and integrity.

ACKNOWLEDGEMENTS

———————————————●———————————————

Chicago, Illinois provides more compelling basketball stories than any city in the world. I am grateful to all the coaches who have contributed to this extraordinary culture. Rick Malnati, Steve Pappas, and Gene Pingatore represent the very best and have candidly and genuinely shared a collective understanding about excellence in teaching. I thank the many voices that helped paint the portrait of my dear friend Steve Pappas. I hope readers will appreciate the eloquent story-telling ability of Cathie Pappas in particular.

Dr. Norman Weston and the Educational Leadership Program at National Louis University challenged me to fight for social justice through educational reform and to learn from the many leaders who continue to champion the cause for empowerment through education.

Dr. Michael Riggle and my colleagues at Glenbrook North High School inspire me to continually examine strategies toward the betterment of the learning experience. Thanks to Robin Pehlke, Jud Gerbich, Jim Quinn, Sue Eddington, and Austin Scott for their artistic contributions.

My deceased parents Leo George Pryma and Margaret Mary McCarthy Pryma emphasized the critical importance of education in our family. I am grateful for their unwavering confidence.

My daughter Jane continues to inspire us with grace, humor, compassion, and unyielding commitment toward equality for all. With love and appreciation, I thank my wife, Marjorie, who has accompanied me through many adventures for over three decades. Laughter truly is the best medicine.

TABLE OF CONTENTS

CHAPTER ONE

INTRODUCTION

Basketball is in my blood. I am smitten by the complexity of this simple game. For decades, the court has been my home and I have enjoyed the privilege of teaching, coaching, and learning from some of the most influential artists (players and coaches) the world has ever known. Chicago, Illinois, for reasons yet to be understood, seems to have developed a disproportionate percentage of this nation's most accomplished artists. It may be its gritty Westside toughness, prairie flatland, blustery Lake Michigan gusts, cultural and architectural form and function, or simply hungry, sweat-drenched, and impoverished cagers violently dancing on shards of glass and asphalt, attacking naked and bent steel rims under the intermittent haze of neon street lamps long after curfew. The underpinnings of this phenomenon rest upon generations of Chicago competitors, maniacally committed warriors who carefully examine the game for all its possibilities.

These competitors sought innovative advantages to gain an edge over neighboring rival innovators. The coaches I selected for this study, Rick Malnati, Gene Pingatore, and Steve Pappas, are each lifelong learners who have bolstered their personal treasuries of understanding with wisdom gleaned from their predecessors, many of whom have been credited with the modernization of the city game. Frequently, my personal esteem was rocked by shameful feelings of inadequacy when attempting to match wits with these savants. Even in victory, long after post-game remarks, perfunctory local newspaper interviews, and bumpy bus rides home, the haunting reality of being out-prepared, outcoached, and most painfully out-performed fueled my relentless compulsion toward perfection. These gifted coaches forced me to improve, and as I evolved, coaches with whom I competed were pressured to evolve as well.

The Power of Coaching

I am intrigued by the sheer power and influence that prominent coaches wield within their schools. In many communities, the high school basketball coach is the most visible and most scrutinized school official. Whether good or bad, these coaches and their persona are on display and are carefully observed by students, parents, staff, alumni, rival communities, and the thousands of fans who support their teams. Some coaches revel in the limelight. Others tolerate the spotlight for the incomparable access to students' minds, hearts, and souls that coaching provides. In either case, coaches and their behaviors reflect the values and expectations of the institutions they represent. Basketball in particular, a communal game that demands skill, thought, and athleticism in a forum reliant upon team play and free expression, provides a willing educational leader the opportunity to motivate young thinkers to examine their lives past and present as well as nudge and prepare these scholar athletes toward the challenges and possibilities ahead.

Sadly, upon decades of observing high school basketball, I continue to marvel at the shallow and all-too-often abusive fits of virulent bombasticity that plague our sidelines and invade the evaluative minds of our youth. Educator Haim Ginott wrote:

> I've come to a frightening conclusion that I am the decisive element in the classroom. It's my personal approach that creates the climate. It's my daily mood that makes the weather. As a teacher, I possess a tremendous power to make a child's life miserable or joyous. I can be a tool of torture or an instrument of inspiration. I can humiliate or humor, hurt or heal. In all situations, it is my response that decides whether a crisis will be escalated or deescalated and a child humanized or dehumanized.

Overexposed media images of collegiate and professional ranting lunatics and narcissistic bullies have damaged not only the integrity of our profession but more insidiously has shaped the conduct and modus operandi of many young coaches, while desensitizing students and parents who tacitly tolerate this abuse. Fortunately, the majority of prep coaches are firmly grounded in educational philosophy. They understand that coaching two to three hours per day, including weekends, travel, and most important, a motivated and captive audience, provides the aforementioned access to students as well as the commensurate responsibilities that classroom teachers rarely approach. These coaches agonize over fastidious decision making while constructing basketball curriculum, program vision, skill development, in-season and off-season calendars, and most critically, strategies to build strong, thoughtful, and courageous men and women.

Rationale

My reason for sharing these stories is simple—I am fascinated by the impact that each of these coaches has provided his community. I selected three Chicago coaches who for decades had shaped the lives of thousands. I sought to learn their magic, document their wisdom, and provide an archive for present day and future coaches who choose to emulate these champions.

The Question

What can we learn from the stories of these extraordinary coaches that will help us to become more insightful teachers and confident leaders?

Five people live and share an unusual communion: achieving unity but not at the expense of individual imagination. You are really betting on the human spirit as much as on mechanical skills. In a day when many workers get paid eight hours' wages for six hours' work, when many politicians ignore the needs of their constituents, and when a lot of policemen fail to show up for a black-out emergency call, why should basketball players be any different? A few will loaf, but the contrast between

> them and members of a well-blended team is stark. Those
> who have ever played on a **team** never forget the excitement
> of their work or the fulfillment of a championship. Those who
> have watched on the night of a final game must sense that
> they have witnessed ultimate cooperation, that they have seen
> an unusual kind of sharing, that they have glimpsed a better
> world—one unattainable outside the arena.

As Senator Bradley stated above, team basketball inspires an "unusual kind of sharing" that at times leads to a better world. The subjects of my study distinguished themselves as master teachers who actively employed their skills toward the betterment of our world. They understood the profound influence they wielded within their respective communities. Immediately, they strove to help students navigate the murky and eventful waters of high school, but their more genuine purpose resided in the future when their prodigies would parlay those resonant lessons learned long ago in a gymnasium into actions that may inspire a better tomorrow.

Most head coaches ascend because they have a proven track record of success in their careers. In high school coaching, careers are defined by one's "real job"—*teaching*. Strong classroom teaching exacts 50-hour weeks that include lesson planning, materials preparation, paper grading, professional development, communication with parents and students, discipline issue follow-up, the tutoring of struggling students, faculty meetings, and actual class time. Strong basketball coaches tack on nearly 40 more hours that include practice planning, facilities and equipment procuring, scouting, film breakdown, mentoring, interviewing, orchestrating college recruitment, traveling, game planning, and actual practice and game time. In a seven-day week comprised of 168 human hours, no wonder high school coaches who work 80 plus hours are exhausted, struggle to maintain healthy families, and fail to stay fit themselves. Pile on the emotional stress associated with constant scrutiny, the agony of defeat, and volatile issues like playing time disagreement and parental unhappiness, the life of a high school coach is taxing.

The grueling basketball season, comprised of 18 dark winter weeks, assaults its victims. The grind is visibly pronounced in coaches' gaunt visages and audible in their painfully hoarse voices. By February, the odyssey of the season has all but physically and mentally defeated these warriors. It is a profession that tests one's sanity. Team USA Coach, Mike Krzyzewski, compared coaching to artistry:

> When a leader is constantly in the public eye, it is tempting to let the media determine whether his team is as great or as bad as they are made out to be. It's like the sculptor or painter, who has to block out what other people say about his work. You may get good suggestions, but ultimately, you have to paint for yourself.

Coaching is often, I repeat, *often* lonely. As competent and assertive as assistants may be, every single decision that steers a team rests with the head coach. Over time many opposing coaches become close friends because they are part of an exclusive fraternity that specifically wrestles with similar issues; but even this resource offers little comfort when a coach's team, *his* organization, *his* program, *his* vision, *his* system of play, *his* identity heads south to territories known as slumps, rebuilding years, and losing seasons. How do coaches survive these ebbs and lulls? Where do they turn when things go awry?

CHAPTER TWO

———————————————•———————————————

LEADERSHIP AND RESEARCH

While amassing, analyzing, and sorting the literature written about leadership, I was struck by a number of recurring themes. Business experts, educational leaders, policy makers, and coaches all must respect the power of these eight identified themes: (a) *courage*, (b) *ambition*, (c) *visioning*, (d) *relationship building*, (e) *communication*, (f) *teaching*, (g) *standing for integrity*, and (h) *inspiring hope*. This chapter will study these themes through the perspectives of varying lenses.

Leaders as Courageous Individuals

Thoreau reflected on the essence of living:

> I went to the woods because I wished to live deliberately, to front only the essential facts of life, and see if I could not learn what it had to teach, and not, when I came to die, discover that I had not lived. I did not wish to live what was not life, living is so dear; nor did I wish to practice resignation, unless it was quite necessary. I wanted to live deep and suck out all the marrow of life, to live so sturdily and Spartan-like as to put to rout all that was not life, to cut a broad swath and shave close, to drive life into a corner, and reduce it to its lowest terms, and, if it proved to be mean, why then to get the whole and genuine meanness of it, and publish its meanness to the world; or if it were sublime, to know it by experience, and be able to give a true account of it in my next excursion.

The urgency, honesty, and passion described by Thoreau prior to his journey into the unknown are qualities firing in the hearts and minds of all courageous *individuals* who accept the challenge to lead. I purposefully selected the noun *individuals* to articulate observations I developed about leadership while reviewing the literature. No two individuals lead their organizations the same way. General Electric's Jack Welch and Intel's Andy Grove have achieved similar results through dissimilar methods. Coach Vince Lombardi's visceral gesticulations starkly contrasted with Coach Tom Landry's placid calculations, yet both empowered their people to championships. Principal David Hagstrom's "aw-shucks"-Andy Griffith approach at Denali school was every bit as inspiring as school superintendent Tony Alvarado's smash mouth, General Patton-style in New York. Whatever your philosophy, Apple's Steve Jobs provided good advice to people who choose to make a difference: "Your time is limited, so don't waste it living someone else's life".

Anatomy of a Leader/Why We Lead

Many choose to lead for the power to run the meetings, set agenda, and be the boss. Coach Gary Barnett argued that these intentions are inappropriate and shallow: "It's not the lot of the leader to be served, but rather it's a privilege to serve." The trappings of leadership are alluring, but cruel reality slapped us all in the head when we crossed the threshold into leadership; as songwriter Bob Dylan astutely wrote, "You've got to serve somebody." The epiphany for many leaders is how selfless we must become to effectively steward our ships. "Leaders of high performing systems put in extraordinary amounts of time. They work hard. They demonstrate that they care. Their consciousness is dominated by the issues and events in the system of which they are a part," asserts Thomas Sergiovanni. All personal plans become secondary at best for leaders of vibrant and dynamic teams.

> Leaders of high performing systems have very strong feelings
> about the attainment of the system's purposes. They care deeply
> about the system. This includes its structure and conduct, its

> history, and its future security. They care deeply about the
> people in the system. They want the system to be successful.
> They want the system to make a respected contribution to
> society. They want the system to contribute to the quality of life
> of people who are involved in it. Their feelings are evidenced
> in the way they talk about the system and in the way in which
> they behave in the system. (Sergiovanni)

That being so, leading an organization, a team or a classroom is a fascinating task that invites unparalleled adventure, once the leader becomes comfortable with the awesome burden of responsibility. Larry Cuban articulated this very well:

> Teaching has also spilled over to the rest of my life. I look
> everywhere for lessons that can be taught and learned. I
> approach situations and think, How can I get my point across?
> What can I learn from this person? My wife and daughters
> have had to endure the questions, the pauses, the indirect
> and direct teaching style over dinner, during vacations, and
> pillow talk.

School leaders, particularly coaches, must accept that their lives will be hijacked due to the intense commitment required in tending to a learning community.

Coaching and Vision

Organizations require just that, **organization**. Visit any community and in an instant one can measure the health of its leadership. I'm inspired by the words of educator, Gordon Donaldson, "It mobilizes members to *think, believe, and behave in a manner that satisfies emerging organizational needs, not simply their individual needs or wants.* When leadership is present, we can detect it in the synchronicity of members' thoughts, words, actions, and outcomes."

Healthy schools share an intense loyalty to progress:

> We know excellent schools when we experience them, despite difficulties in definition. In excellent schools things "hang together," a sense of purpose rallies people to a common cause, work as meaning and life is significant, teachers and students work together and with spirit, and accomplishments are readily recognized. (Sergiovanni)

Yet, these accomplishments are short lived, and the visionary must be mindful that today's action builds tomorrow's experiences. "A good leader has to look beyond what his team is doing now—or there could be serious consequences down the road. Whatever a leader does now sets up what he does later. And there's always a later" (Krzyzewski)

Innate intelligence, intuitive familiarity with group dynamics, pragmatic deployment of resources, and flexible understanding of synergy within systems are all prerequisites for the mindful leader. According to Longenecker and Pinkel:

> Some people believe that being an effective coach is simply the ability to motivate people (e.g. give good pep talks, challenge and inspire others). Yet, motivating people is only part of the key role of a coach. The modern day coach in both sports and business must also create a "performance system" that enables people to perform effectively.

Achieving harmony in this "performance system" may appear complex, but it is founded in simple principles, as was discovered by the great Bear Bryant:

> I'm just a plow-hand from Arkansas, but I have learned how to hold a team together. You have to lift some up, and calm others down, until finally they've got one heartbeat together. That's all it takes to get people to win.

A visionary must embrace, no, **revel** in chaos, change, uncertainty, and the fickle and frail elements of human nature. As Emotional Intelligence guru Daniel Goleman suggested, "Leadership is not domination, but the art of persuading people to work toward a common goal." This art of persuasion underscores the critical value of genuine relationships within an actively participatory community.

Coach-Athlete Compatibility

Legendary NFL football coach Vince Lombardi possessed incredible humanity in his responsibility to his players. Coach Lombardi stated:

> The strength of the group is in the strength of the leader. Many mornings when I am worried or depressed, I have to give myself what is almost a pep talk, because I am not going before that ball club without being able to exude assurance. I must be the first believer, because there is no way you can hoodwink the players.

These findings appear obvious; yet, why are playing fields and courts littered with coaching behaviors that brazenly irritate the wounds of injured esteems? Systems analyst Peter Senge suggested: "Pushing harder, whether through an increasingly aggressive intervention or through increasingly stressful withholding of natural instincts, is exhausting. Yet, as individuals and organizations, we not only get drawn into compensating feedback, we often glorify the suffering that ensues." Demand for constant improvement is not an excuse for an impatient coach who damages the will of his troops in the name of fortitude. Business leader Dan Robertson acknowledged the transcendence of coaching tenets into business practice:

> Coaching is a vital ingredient to the success of any leader. A leader must be able to coach their subordinates without stooping to intimidation and fear. An effective coach educates mentors and motivates his team while developing a team

strategy and game plan, accompanied by achievable goals and objectives. The coach sets the foundation by creating an environment of understanding and trust, which in-turn leads to outstanding ethical behavior by the team in applying business practices.

NBA coach Phil Jackson confidently preached the value of a trusting environment: "Find a structure that would empower everybody, not just the stars. And allow the players to grow as individuals as they surrender themselves to the group effort."

How do gifted leaders emerge equipped with the confidence to stifle their own egos in order to nurture the growth of their players? Eastern philosopher Lao-Tsu offered *simplicity* as the answer to this question:

A leader is best when people barely know he exists. Not so good when people obey and acclaim him. Worse when they despise him. But of a good leader who talks little when his work is done, his aim fulfilled they will say "We did it ourselves."

Phil Jackson, an ardent student of spiritual freedom, added:

In Zen it is said that the gap between accepting things and the way they are and wishing them to be otherwise is "the tenth of an inch of difference between heaven and hell." If we can accept whatever hand we've been dealt—no matter how unwelcome— the way to proceed eventually becomes clear. This is what is meant by right action: the capacity to observe what's happening and act appropriately, without being distracted by self-centered thoughts. If we rage and resist, our angry, fearful minds have trouble quieting down sufficiently to allow us to act in the most beneficial way for ourselves and others."

Despite our best intentions, we often struggle to be levelheaded when driving people toward organizational excellence. Coach Lombardi admitted:

"Like my father before me, I have a violent temper with which I have been struggling all my life, and with which I have had to effect compromise. It is ineradicable, but it must not be irrational." Donaldson agreed with Lombardi and Jackson:

> Underlying our capacity to foster relationships are two other
> qualities: our success at forming authentic relationships
> ourselves and, in turn, our own intrapersonal self-awareness.
> We need to understand ourselves well enough to gauge
> accurately how our behaviors will be received by others and
> then, be skilled at consultation with others to discuss and
> mediate feelings of fear, uncertainty, and even hostility that
> our behaviors might provoke.

The coach as nurturer is basic; yet, the self-discipline required to consistently nurture, especially through crises, eludes many leaders. It was at these times of crises that school principal, David Hagstrom learned the importance of affirmation and said, "William Stafford had gone on to tell me, 'You need to honor your organization, and honor each person who dwells in the place that you call a school.'" Revered basketball coach, John Wooden, offered ten positive affirmations for each criticism and enlisted his team managers to monitor his pattern in the interest of upbeat and productive practice sessions. Like Jack Welch of General Electric, Bob Wall challenged managers to openly evaluate their people and approach these evaluations as John Wooden would have:

> Leaders should increase the amount of praise they offer to staff.
> The infrequency of praise from leaders has always mystified
> me. People want nothing more than to do a good job and be
> recognized for it. Most leaders acknowledge they should give
> more positive feedback. Yet a recent Gallup Poll revealed that
> 65 percent of Americans haven't received recognition in the
> past year. A United States Department of Labor study found
> that the number one reason why people leave organizations
> is that they don't feel appreciated. The Gallup study found

that increasing employee recognition lowers turnover, raises customer loyalty, and increases productivity.

Feedback doesn't need to be complimentary as long as it is genuine. "Specificity," Levinson (1992) (as cited in Goleman, 1995) pointed out, "is just as important for praise as it is for criticism. I won't say that vague praise has no effect at all, but it doesn't have much, and you can't learn from it."

The Art of Communication

The simplest question can harvest a paradigm shift, as David Hagstrom learned as a principal in Alaska when he asked: "What do you want for your children, here at Denali School?" His simple question opened doors that had been closed for decades and when he proved his sincerity, an entire community rallied to lift the children. As Professor Richard Elmore observed, "The problems of the system are the problems of the smallest unit." We often overlook basic evidence while we wrestle with enormous issues. Communication reveals the smallest units in the system and will often lead to what Hall of Famer Red Auerbach professed to his Celtics: "That's what it all comes down to, in my mind anyway: A matter of respect. That's always been important to me."

Respectful and open communication may lead to unexpected and perhaps threatening candor. According to Phil Jackson,

Many coaches are control-oholics. They keep a tight rein on everyone from the players to the equipment manager, and set strict guidelines for how each person should perform. Everything flows from the top, and the players dare not think for themselves. That approach may work in isolated cases, but it usually only creates resentment."

Often, this resentment stems from a power struggle fueled by a leader's fear of usurpation. Leaders must respect the words of Robert Frost, "nothing gold can stay," while accepting the ubiquitous nature of change. Educational reformer Tony Wagner noted:

> Living in the midst of rapid change, most of us have a hard time
> truly seeing its essential features. But if we are to understand
> more deeply what students need to know and be able to do, as
> well as what kind of schools will be most helpful to them, then
> we must first consider how a changing world is shaping today's
> young people and their future."

As people confront a challenge and share ideas, collective confidence is born. Why do leaders resist opportunities to build collective confidence? "Mutual commitment helps overcome the fear of failure—especially when people are part of a team sharing and achieving goals. It also sets the stage for open dialogue and honest conversation" (Wagner)

Coach Krzyzewski shared his position on communication and the leader's relationships:

> I've been forming teams since I was a kid in Chicago. It's
> what I enjoy most in life. It's what I do. Almost everything in
> leadership comes back to relationships. And, naturally, the
> level of cooperation on any team increases tremendously as the
> level of trust rises. The only way you can possibly lead people
> is to understand people. And the best way to understand them
> is to get to know them better.

Coach Krzyzewski's interpersonal skill set served Duke Basketball powerfully. His willingness to hone his communicative style separated him from his contemporaries, but as Goleman revealed, Coach Krzyzewski was at the front of a trend:

> As Shoshona Zuboff, a psychologist at Harvard Business
> School, pointed out to me, "corporations have gone through a
> radical revolution within this century, and with this has come
> a corresponding transformation of the emotional landscape.
> There was a long period of managerial domination of the
> corporate hierarchy when the manipulative, jungle-fighter

boss was rewarded. But that rigid hierarchy started breaking down in the 1980s under the twin pressures of globalization and information technology. The jungle fighter symbolizes where the corporation has been; the virtuoso in interpersonal skills is the corporate future."

Coaching and Professional Mentoring

Team building has become synonymous with professional development toward a learning community. Soccer Coach Tony DiCicco understood the power of team: "The objective in any team sport is to transform the group from a mere collection of talented individuals into a highly cohesive unit so that the whole is greater than the sum of its parts."

Educational leaders, particularly principals, have tapped into the value of teamwork as well as the critical importance of building a team comprised of diverse skills striving toward one common goal. "The single most important factor in maximizing the excellence of a group's product was the degree to which the members were able to create a state of internal harmony, which lets them take advantage of the full talent of their members."(Goleman) Donaldson added to Goleman's thoughts on harmony and synergy: "As with sport, the most productive organizational action is not identical, uniform and lock-stepped. Action-in-common results from the voluntary choreography of many individual efforts, calling upon the idiosyncratic talents and characters of each person."

"In mid-season, do you want a team that runs good plays or a team of players with good skills?" As rudimentary as Coach Don Meyer's question is, educational experts concur; developing skills in teachers will pay much greater dividends than almost any other school improvement initiative.

The emphasis on a learning community with teachers as models and the galvanizing bond that fortifies when people experience new learning together mirrors the evolution of exceptional athletic teams.

There have been studies that show that exceptional swimmers are actually faster when they swim 100 meters as part of a relay team than when they are in an individual race. It seems that as a part of a team an athlete gathers support from the other team members, which makes the individual better. In other words, as a part of the whole, performances are raised, and that's the relay paradigm. The effective coach nurtures these performances enhancing team relationships so that the team's performance is better than the sum of its players' talent and coach's leadership. (Dicicco & Hacker)

Duke University's Mike Krzyzewski believed that most people hunger for opportunities to work together and stated: "People want to be on a team. They want to be part of something bigger than themselves. They want to be in a situation where they feel that they are doing something for the greater good." The trick is for the coach to provide an atmosphere of trust and encouragement that invites learners to stumble and, in some cases, fall while attempting to better themselves which in turn will better the entire team (learning community). John Heider offered this analogy of leadership:

The wise leader is like water. Consider water: water cleanses and refreshes all creatures without distinction and without judgment: water freely and fearlessly goes deep beneath the surface of things: water is fluid and responsive; water follows the law freely.

Consider the leader: the leader works in any setting without complaint, with any person or issue that comes on the floor; the leader acts so that all will benefit and serves well regardless of the rate of pay; the leader speaks simply and honestly and intervenes in order to shed light and create harmony.

Leaders who respect Heider's analogy to water will naturally develop powerful teamwork.

Coaching and the Inevitability of Change

"If you put a plant in a jar, it will take the shape of the jar. But if you allow the plant to grow freely, twenty jars might not be able to hold it." (Krzyzewski) Duke teams exuded growth and creativity. Another champion of change, Miami Heat coach Pat Riley, espoused a theory about thunderbolts. A good coach expects the occasional thunderbolt, catastrophic injury, personal drama or more positively, an advantageous acquisition or help from an unexpected source. Every once in a while, Coach Riley and Coach Jackson agreed:

> Like life, basketball is messy and unpredictable. It has its way with you, no matter how hard you try to control it. The trick is to experience each moment with a clear mind and open heart. When you do that, the game—and life—will take care of itself.

Peter Senge wrote:

> Systems thinking is a discipline for seeing wholes. It is a framework for seeing interrelationships rather than things, for seeing patterns of change rather than static "snapshots." It is a set of general principles—distilled over the course of the twentieth century, spanning fields as diverse as the physical and social sciences, engineering and management.

Assuming Senge, Jackson, Riley, and Krzyzewski are accurate in their assessments, a team can't improve *unless* it changes.

The very premise of competitive sport is founded on the desire for change. Faster, stronger, smarter, tougher, better timing, more unified, more intense, more diverse, more harmonious are all concepts discussed every day in practice. Coaching leaders must model their affinity for growth and change. "If only the principal will grow, the school will grow. To change something, someone has to change first." (Barth) Educational theorist Roland Barth intimated why so many leaders eschew genuine change: "Another serious impediment to the principal as a learner is that by engaging publicly in learning we openly admit imperfection" and further implored, "The most powerful reason for principals to be learners as well as leaders comes from the extraordinary influence of modeling behavior. Do as I do as well as I say is a winning formula."

Leaders who celebrate change are those who will inspire their people to confidently pursue excellence. Phil Jackson wrote about preparing one's mind for change:

> The meditation practice we teach players is called *mindfulness*. To become mindful, one must cultivate what Suzuki Roshi calls "beginner's mind," an "empty" state free from limiting self-centered thoughts. If your mind is empty, Roshi wrote in *Zen Mind, Beginner's Mind*, it is always ready for anything; it is open to everything. In the beginner's mind there are many possibilities; in the expert's mind there are few."

Coaching and Morality

Sergiovanni spoke of the potential for learning communities that embrace teamwork:

> The web of relationships that stand out in communities are different in kind than those found in more gesellschaft organizations. They are more special, meaningful, and personalized. They result in a quality of connectedness that has moral overtones. In addition, because of these overtones, members feel a special sense of obligation to look out for each other.

Ed Monahan, golf coach at St. Ignatius College Prep, penetrated the reptilian brains of his players by incessantly repeating, "Once you alter the rules, golf ceases to be a game." Ed, like any coach worth his salt, recognized that schools support extra-curricula in large part because they provide hands-on life lessons, many of which are developmental primers toward a more ethical society. In this regard, Coach Wooden suggested:

The coach must never forget that he is a leader and not merely a person with authority. The youngsters under his supervision must be able to receive proper guidance from him in all respects and not merely in regard to the proper playing of the game of basketball.

John Wooden is arguably the most successful coach in American history; yet, his motives often downplayed victory in exchange for moral learning:

Next to their parents, youngsters spend more time with and are more likely to be influenced by their teachers than anyone else, and the coach is the teacher who will provide by far the most influence. Therefore, it is not only the duty but also the obligation of the coach to be fully aware of and to handle this responsibility with grave concern. The powerful influence of example should be a sacred trust for all of those who are in the position to help mold the character of young people in their formative years.

Our American democratic society, like sport, is weakened by a lack of integrity. The achievements of Barry Bonds, Mark McGuire, and Sammy Sosa will forever be dubious. Teachers and students who doctor test scores are missing the point. Enron and World Com have become institutions of iconic infamy. School leader John Larson commented on the contribution high school athletics can make in developing integrity:

From my observation as a coach, as an athletic official and as a school administrator, I believe that athletics in our high schools, properly handled help to develop good citizenship. They tend to teach fair play and good sportsmanship. They foster respect for the worth of the individual regardless of his race creed or economic background. They develop team spirit and the importance of carrying out individual assignments as part of and essential to team success.

Coaching a simple game mindfully will yield lifelong lessons.

> On the surface this may sound like a crazy idea, but intuitively I sensed that there was a link between spirit and sport. Besides, winning at *any* cost didn't interest me. From my years as a member of the championship New York Knicks, I'd already learned that winning is ephemeral. Yes, victory is sweet, but it doesn't necessarily make life any easier the next season or even the next day. After the cheering crowds disperse and the last bottle of champagne is drained, you have to return to the battlefield and start all over again. (Phil Jackson)

Coaching Coaches

Professional Development has finally emerged as the core element in school improvement. Coaching teachers to perform more powerfully, and ultimately independently, is the goal. According to businessman Jim Collins, "True leadership only exists if people follow when they have the freedom not to." Like most coaches, Collins is probably familiar with the Kipling line, "For the strength of the Pack is in the Wolf, and the strength of the Wolf is the Pack." The pack and the wolf relationship requires all members of a team to become mindful leaders:

> Essentially the leader's task is consciousness-raising on a wide plane.... The leader's fundamental act is to induce people to be aware or conscious of what they feel—to feel their true needs so strongly, to define their values so meaningfully, that they can be moved to purposeful action. (Donaldson)

Dean Michael Fullan must have interviewed tired and frustrated coaches when he wrote, "An organization cannot flourish—at least not for long—on the actions of the top leader alone." Fullan continued to stress the importance of "the pack" for its future implications: "To a certain extent, a school's leader's effectiveness in creating a culture of sustained change will be determined by the leaders he or she leaves behind." Fullan and Donaldson were concerned about sustaining evolved systems. They insisted that it is incumbent upon leaders to build future leaders. Coaching is much easier when surrounded by player/coaches (participants who also orchestrate). "Our past understanding of school leadership has failed to meet two functional tests in recent decades: that it successfully promotes organizational improvement and that it be sustainable for the leaders themselves" (Donaldson)

Coaches must invite players to see "big picture" and exhort them to become active decision makers in all matters relevant to the future direction of the team. I'm reminded of the work of former Purdue coach Gene Keady. He delegated major responsibilities to his players. One player was responsible and held accountable for team free throw proficiency, another for offensive rebound attack, and so on. He believed that this ownership would engage investment at a much deeper level. His record suggests he was onto something, but the proof of the pudding is in the successful lives of his former players, many in their forties, who credit those "Keady" responsibilities for teaching them about genuine collaboration.

Coaching and Teaching

According to educational reformer Deborah Meier, "Teaching more than virtually any activity (aside from parenting, perhaps) depends on quick instinctive habits and behavior, and on deeply held ways of seeing and valuing." Meier could just as easily be describing coaching or leadership. John Wooden revered his role as teacher:

> The coach must be a teacher. He must understand the learning processes and follow the laws of learning. He must be able to explain and provide a demonstration, have the players imitate the proper demonstration, constructively criticize and correct their demonstration, and have the corrected imitation repeated and repeated until the proper execution becomes automatic.

Strong teachers understand Multiple Intelligence Theory and design learning opportunities to meet the needs of students. Coaches rely on similar strategies. *Talk, Chalk, and Walk* is an age old method to lecture information such as a drill or play, draw the drill on the board, and walk through the drill in rehearsal prior to executing the learning sequence kinesthetically at full tilt.

Like teachers, coaches carefully design a thriving learning environment, a relevant and stimulating curriculum, and basic expectations for optimal use of time and space. Larry Cuban inspired and reflected:

> In teaching, I have experienced the deep satisfactions of connecting to others in ineffable moments, producing odd tingles, even goosebumps on my back and neck, when a class, small group, or individual and I become one—moments listening to students that provided me with an insight that upended a conventional idea, moments that forced me to rethink after I had closed my mind's door, moments when my students had touched me deeply. These rare instances are like the resounding crack of a bat that sends a ball soaring into left field or like the graceful pivot to avoid the outstretched arms of an opposing player that allows you to go for an easy lay-up. These moments I treasure.

A strong curriculum works towards mastery-learning, incorporating elements of repetition, leading to consistency, and building to discovery of more sophisticated concepts. Most high school coaches rely heavily on the pedagogical training they received as developing educators. Like Wooden, coaches perceive themselves as teachers first, but understand that the lure of the game awakens their students more easily than traditional class work:

> That's when I come alive: on the basketball court. As the game unfolds, time slows down and I experience the blissful feeling of being totally engaged in the action. One moment I may crack a joke and the next cast a woeful look at a ref. But all the

while I'm thinking: how many timeouts do we have left? Who needs to get going out there on court? What's up with my guys on the bench? My mind is completely focused on the goal, but with a sense of openness and joy. (Phil Jackson)

Intuitive coaches parlay an athlete's passionate connection to the game into leverage that will nudge that athlete to transfer athletic understanding to life experience.

Block scheduling, two hour practices each day, provide additional advantage to the coach who utilizes his resources prudently. School Reform activist, Tony Wagner insisted that now more than ever, after-school programs are essential to American children: "Only about 5 percent of adolescents' time was spent with a parent or parents—and a disproportionate amount of that time was with their mothers." A coach accepts a unique role in modern society and, according to Wagner, the dependency upon coach/athlete relationships must proliferate to address the need. "The conclusion from this data is inescapable: young people today are growing up profoundly alone—perhaps more than at any time in human history. They are being raised by each other, as much as by anyone."

Hope

Imagine Dr. Martin Luther King as a coach or school leader. He often shared a comparison that one could live for days without food, hours without water, and minutes without air, but one cannot live a second without hope. Through this research, I was struck by the prolific recurrence of the word hope. Sergiovanni emphasized the power of hope in leadership: "But too often, hope is overlooked or misunderstood. Modern management theory tells us that the only results that count are those you can see and compute." Sergiovanni continued: "Leaders of hopeful school communities recognize the potential in people and in situations." "General Colin Powell says he would almost always choose to follow the unrealistic aspirations of an optimist than the often grim views of a realist." (Zinn) Donna Carroll of Dominican University lives by these rules in her role as president and was quoted as saying, "Absorb chaos; give back calm; provide hope."

Summary

Athletes would relish the opportunity to play for Jim Collins because he respected the democratic underpinnings of team building:

> In legislative leadership, on the other hand, no individual leader—not even the nominal chief executive—has enough structural power to make the most important decisions by himself or herself. Legislative leadership relies more upon persuasion, political currency, and shared interests to create the conditions for the right decisions to happen.

As business thinking encroaches upon the delivery of American education, I am struck by the influence that coaching has had on business. Educational leaders have just begun to tap into concepts like learning teams, learning styles, and community goals. Outside on the sandlots as well as in the gymnasiums right there on American school grounds, these concepts have been emphasized for well over a century. As distasteful as the encroachment of business models exerted on education may be, the sourness is mitigated slightly from the satisfaction that many of these business models were shaped from the minds of coaches. Fortunately teachers and coaches recognize the sanity in Reeves' words:

> Educational leaders who view the students as customers accept a world of superficiality, mediocrity, instant gratification, and as a result, popularity. Educational leaders who reject this view risk their short-term popularity but remain true to their values. They replace superficiality with depth, mediocrity with excellence, and instant gratification with appreciation years in the future.

In Chapter Two, I researched the thinking on coaching and its relationship with courage, ambition, vision, compatibility, communication, teaching, organizational leadership, morality, sustainability, and finally hope. Once again, the words of Thomas Sergiovanni provide our educational leadership community with its most critical imperative: "Instead of importing theories and practices from business, we should be inventing our own." As we invent our own theories and practices, my hope is that elements of coaching will be inextricably included.

CHAPTER THREE

———————————————●———————————————

BRIEF BUT IMPORTANT METHODOLOGY

U ncovering and understanding the genius of these educational leaders was one step. Organizing, analyzing, and accurately articulating their collective genius escalated the step to that of a leap or a bound. This chapter reveals the strategies I employed to achieve both step and leap while sharing gritty insights about the Chicago Basketball World.

What can we learn from the stories of these extraordinary coaches
that will help us to become more mindful teachers and confident leaders?

To capture the depth of their acumen, I brought to this study decades of my own teaching and coaching experience. Year after year I pursued clarity, efficiency, and inspiration. We teachers execute thousands of decisions each day. What distinguishes the daily lessons of these three accomplished teachers? Why do their students (players) consistently demonstrate mastery in even the most sophisticated schemes? How did these masters arrive at their philosophical standing, what lessons have they learned along the way, and what elements of their arsenal separate them from mediocrity? My daunting challenge was to weave my personal observations collected over time, documented historical record, and the stories told by these visionaries into a balanced, systematic, and harmonious tapestry of useful information that will help to shape the thinking of other educators and leaders.

For instance, how did Steve Pappas imbue the sense of humanity and brotherhood so vibrantly into his lessons? Why did Rick Malanati's teams perform with supreme confidence? How did "Ping" continue to relate so effectively with students after fifty years in the profession?

RESEARCH DESIGN
Narrative Methodology

This study is reliant upon the findings harvested through conversations with each of the subjects. When conducted properly, these conversations based upon the subjects' lives led to telling, retellings, and ultimately narratives.

This study is a compilation of three separate series of interviews. Sixteen interview questions (see Appendix A) were winnowed from an original list of 45 questions so as to optimize responses. Each subject required a minimum of five hours of actual recorded interviews. The interviews were then transcribed verbatim. The transcriptions were carefully read, categorized, and prioritized. I selected elements from the transcriptions that best captured the essence of the subjects. This selection phase of the research proved to be daunting. Unfortunately, many colorful exchanges and asides are not included in this book in an effort to provide the reader with a product of familiarity and continuity. In other words, there were far too many stories.

Interviewing

Each of the subjects was audio recorded. The conversations were then transcribed. I chose to retain authentic language when possible, recognizing the raw and unpolished nature of some of the responses. That rawness helped to modify the subjects' stories and provided these narratives with humanity.

While analyzing the recorded data, I chose, when possible, to arrange the narratives complementarily, beginning with the subjects' early years, their mentors, influences, and then proceeding into their methodologies and philosophies. I allowed their own voices to interpret the data, but recognized that in order to avail relevance, I needed to intervene from time to time.

Strategy, Rationale, and Purpose

"Let's change lives today!" Pete Gillen spent decades teaching high school in Brooklyn, New York before "changing lives" at University of Notre Dame, Xavier University, University of Virginia, and Providence College. He would implore us with these words each morning before we worked with the best players in the nation at the 5 Star Basketball Camp in Pittsburgh, Pennsylvania. I have spent my career developing and refining methods to "change lives" as Coach Gillen changed mine as well as thousands of others.

As I approached this study, I was not concerned about statistics. As Bill Veeck, Chicago philosopher turned major league baseball owner, often said, "How much money must you pay a flower to bloom?" Each of these legendary "flowers," the subjects of this study, accumulated hundreds of victories, scores of awards, and heaps of tangible mementos. A quantitative analysis would have revealed a glimmer of how these practitioners "change lives" each day, but the study would have lacked passion, nuance, humor, value, and ultimately, the sweat and blood that build champions. These coaches could have chosen to be millionaires. Instead, they invested their talents in the hope of a better future by nurturing people through the adventures of high school. If chasing records and victories powered their vision, they would have been satisfied years ago.

The flesh and blood nature of qualitative thinking allowed me the freedom and license to dig deep and unearth the gold that resides in these formidable managers. These champions were already proven in the quantifiable world. I sought to learn about the patterns, rituals, and mindfulness of these innovators. A quantitative study would have limited this search.

The bulk of harvested data emanated from interviews with the subjects. I aimed to engender frank conversation about the importance of this game of basketball, its impact in the academic as well as character realms of young people, and ultimately, uncover trade secrets from these cagey veterans in the hope of providing a foundational primer for fellow coaches, teachers, and leaders who strive for excellence. I recognized that my line of questioning required consistency in order to glean strands of similar revelation; but in the early interviews, I learned that much of the richness that I sought evoked from tangential comments and multiple layers of responses mined from a very simple question. For example, after 20 minutes of response to the question, "What are your weaknesses?" Coach Malnati revealed that his ability to connect with troubled kids is directly related to his own esteem issues. As I engaged each subject, I was mindful of consistency in my line of questioning, but celebrated the tangential caroms that led to the gold, as described in Coach Malnati's remarks about troubled kids.

Phenomenologically, coaching high school basketball is truly a world of its own. The subjects in this study devoted 40 plus hours a week to their teams on top of the hours they responsibly contributed as educators toward their curricular duties. How they balance family life, personal health, and spiritual sanity are epic achievements themselves. Add the pressures related to performance, the complex nature of teenagers, and the volatile frailty associated with parental expectations and a coach's life can become a powder keg. I am reminded of the assertion a veteran coach made at a clinic recently, "my paycheck as a coach is in the hands of a seventeen year old." On the other hand, the euphoria derived from a well-played sequence or a well-developed single purposed TEAM offers coaches moments of incomparable satisfaction. We relish walking through town after huge victories, and are haunted by our vilification after huge losses. Our work is open and vulnerable to criticism as President Theodore Roosevelt so eloquently proclaimed:

> It is not the critic who counts; not the man who points out how the strong man stumbles, or where the doer of deeds could have done them better. The credit belongs to the man who is actually in the arena, whose face is marred by dust and sweat and blood, who strives valiantly; who errs and comes short again and again; because there is not effort without error and shortcomings; but who does actually strive to do the deed; who knows the great enthusiasm, the great devotion, who spends himself in a worthy cause, who at the best knows in the end the triumph of high achievement and who at the worst, if he fails, at least he fails while daring greatly. So that his place shall

never be with those cold and timid souls who know neither
victory nor defeat.

As President Roosevelt stated in this 1910 speech titled "Citizenship in a
Republic," we are actively participating and exposed to public criticism. This
lifestyle choice is a phenomenon, a calling, and in some cases an addiction.
My personal coaching background helped me to portray this phenomenon
accurately.

Ethnographically, Chicago high school basketball is a culture of its own. The
traditions of Public League dominance, Catholic League intensity, and suburban
resourcefulness provide a foundation of contrasting styles and stubborn
loyalties. Friday night at Brother Rice, Wednesday afternoon at Farragut, or
any instances where traditional rivals lock horns provide incredible drama,
pageantry, and at times cultural ugliness. Coaches methodically plod through
marathon seasons creating the program calendar; constructing strength and
conditioning off season opportunities; calendaring summer camps, shootouts,
and activities; formulating practice plans and skull sessions; orchestrating
film sessions; communicating with the media; advocating for your players to
capture college attention; coordinating facilities and activities with lower levels,
feeder programs, colleagues who coach other winter sports; communicating
with parents; scouting; preparing game plans; and ultimately coaching on game
night. These activities are just an outline of the real work that glues this culture
together. Along the way, Chicago basketball winds its way through turf wars,
poverty, politics, ethics, and other power struggles reflective of the City of Big
Shoulders.

Of all the elements woven into the fabric of coaching high school basketball
in Chicago, it is this ethnographic piece that taught me the most and that I miss
most dearly since leaving the game. My travel through this great city opened my
eyes to beauty in neighborhoods, ethnicities, architecture, and traditions that I
otherwise would not have encountered. The Black National Anthem was sung
before games at Hales Franciscan. Proviso East's roaring pep band could wake
the dead. Jewish enclaves had a deep affinity for basketball. Glenbrook North

Boosters offered the best concession food, including the "Pieper Special," a marinated steak sandwich named after their beloved football coach. Thornton's official scorer and clock official were perched some 30 feet above courtside. St. Patrick, an all-boys school, had a section deep in the corner reserved for their student fans; this was humorously named the STUD. SECTION and opposing team corner shooters were harassed unmercifully from there. Old Mendel Catholic had perpetual sewer problems—at least in the visitor locker room. The temperature in Waukegan's visitor locker room hovered near 100°F. After dunks at Lincoln Park High School, a reserve player armed with a long pole readjusted the basket to its proper place while play continued. The three point arcs are interrupted by the players' benches in the converted library on the fourth floor of Leo High School that served as their gymnasium. When heavy snow mounted on the dome at Glenbrook South, the basketball standards and rims lowered under the pressure, allowing for highlight- reel dunking on snowy days. Student sections from St. Ignatius, New Trier, and North Side Prep tended to offer the most cerebral unified commentary: "Harass them! Harass them! Make them relinquish the ball!" and "Just like football! Just like soccer! Just like last time! Just like always!"

Neighborhood cuisine helped to motivate coaches to scout on an otherwise rare night off. Coaches, scouts, fans, and referees frequented local establishments after games. De La Salle had Ricobene's or Schaller's Pump. Fenwick had Salernos or Parky's. Whitney Young had Tufanos and the gems of Taylor Street. Leyden had Gene and Jude's. Bluestone in Evanston served the Wildkits and Trevians. These were diners and saloons that stayed open late and allowed for both a good meal and a timely conversation about upcoming opponents.

This ethnographic approach underscores the importance of building strong relationships. Young coaches often underestimate the value of conducting themselves as dignified visitors. Perennial fans, workers, vendors, and beat writers appreciate a class act. Once demonstrated, all kinds of learning avails itself. Conversely, boorish and whining coaches are treated poorly and, in some instances, a poorly timed faux pas could become an irrevocable insult. Coaches must model for their players and communities the value of celebrating a worthy opponent and respecting the loyalty people have for their school teams. The high school basketball culture in Chicago was rich and alive and influenced the way our three extraordinary subjects evolved as educators.

Context

As America adjusts to the many peripheral issues connected to No Child Left Behind and Race to the Top, the emphasis on the failure of educators and their contribution to the achievement gap has all but squelched the stories about successful teaching practice. Literacy enrichment programs, character counts programs, incentive achievement programs, schools within schools, study skills programs, charter schools, corporate schools, specialized academies, and hundreds of other innovative initiatives are at best noble experiments in the name of student achievement and more genuinely unproven theoretical whims to temporarily pacify impatient politicians and school board officials who must answer the complexities surrounding the magic of child development.

Renoir promised to paint only beauty. This study is my attempt to share beautiful stories from these wise practitioners who, despite the flavor of the day paradigms and running scared educational leadership, found their voices and their way and demonstrated tried and true educational excellence for decades. Failing students were rare in the programs directed by these wise educators. Admittedly, they carefully selected student/athletes to their squads which provided them an immediate edge, but why did they consistently flourish in an extra-curricular where so many others struggle? Why did their students thrive in high school, excel through college and professional life, and more often than not return to loyally support the program that helped them on their paths?

In my experience in both public and private schools, many of our strongest teachers developed their skills through coaching. Coaching demands honesty, integrity, and a firm understanding of relationships built upon trust. Success in coaching as in teaching is directly related to the level of investment the teacher has in his or her children. Coaches understand this. I cringe every time an institution selects a teaching candidate with multiple degrees from prestigious schools over the proven teacher/coach who will offer not only dynamic classroom energy, but is not afraid of working well into the evening providing additional enrichment to the entire school community. Sadly, the pedigreed teacher often chooses to close shop at three p.m. each day, or even worse, leaves the school all together after a short experimental stint in search of greener career pastures far, far away from the blue collar nature of inspired teaching.

Interactive teamwork drives the health of all organizations. If public education is truly interested in preparing youth for life and lifelong learning, shouldn't the notion of working with others be a central tenet? Coaching students to share their talents toward a common goal could be a stride toward tolerance, closing the achievement gap, and building democratic principles.

Too often, the work of coaches is relegated to a lesser level of respect in a school community; yet, I have witnessed the impact in overall school climate when talented coaches are welcomed into school leadership roles. This study revealed that good coaching is good teaching, and good teaching is good coaching. A qualitative lens painted a richer portrait of relationships, teamwork, and the humanity present in the art of teaching.

Participants

The Chicago Three who were the subjects in this study were extraordinary educators who happen to be basketball coaches. Their selection was based on simple criteria. Each of them had spent decades honing their skills; achieved significant success; profoundly influenced the direction of their respective communities; and earned the respect of their peers, officials, fans, media, and most important, their students. Simply, I admired them and respected the difference they have made in the world. The participants in this study were:

- Rick Malnati: New Trier High School (Fenwick High School)

- Gene Pingatore: St. Joseph High School

- Steve Pappas: Deerfield High School (Gordon Tech High School)

I was fully cognizant of my affection for each of these subjects and worked to be as unbiased as possible in my research. As I considered the ethical/power issues in this project, I was guided by the notion that these stories must be penned. Current and future teachers/coaches will benefit from the wisdom of the Chicago Three. The participants understood that their words and ideas would be quoted throughout the study.

Assumptions

I saw my role in this research as a preservationist. When landmark buildings are felled, the authenticity of their gifts, shortcomings, and eccentricities are lost without a careful archive. I endeavored to preserve the wisdom that resided in each of these coaches, and compiled a document that genuinely captured their thoughts on leading and teaching and their effects on modern day team building. Each participant was nearing the sunset of his career; therefore, the timing of this study was appropriate and advantageous.

I entered this study with strong convictions about teamwork, selflessness, skill refinement, openness to growth, and goal attainment. Urgency without purpose retards growth. I anticipated these stalwarts would reveal strategies toward balance, energy, and health. My personal familiarity with this domain served as a filter separating and documenting only exceptional thoughts. The work was compelling and instrumental. As much as I intended to be as transparently invisible as possible, I know myself, and amplified unabashedly the concepts that resonated within my own system of beliefs.

Personally, I owed these three Chicago icons my very best work. They have invested their blood, sweat, and time so that the youth on their watch were provided strong models and motivational encouragement to blossom into powerful, thoughtful, and confident citizens.

Summary

The methods I selected to capture the essence of these educational leaders affirmed my decision to approach this study from a qualitative lens. Creswell lauded qualitative research as a "complex, holistic picture." Sport lends itself to quantification, but to unearth the secrets to best practice, I worked beyond the scoreboard. I have always been leery of scoreboards. If 30 years of coaching has taught me anything, it is that the numbers on the scoreboard reveal that the team that chases the numbers most ruthlessly or the team with the most talent typically wins. Scoreboards don't measure the strides taken by losing teams, the richness of the experience, the depth of relationships, the values learned, the skills acquired, or the archiving of the journey a team has traveled to arrive at this place in their evolution. Those last three concepts are educationally related: winning is often bottom-line-driven.

I chose to add the word "ruthless" to describe this bottom-line-driven phenomenon because words like ruthless seem to be antithetical to the learning process; yet, the proliferation of shallow business models spilling into educational initiatives has spawned a new and more measurable vocabulary describing failure in American schools. Failure is measured by numbers. Culturally biased test design, poverty, readiness, generational illiteracy, special education issues, and the basic inability of students to connect with traditional Western influences are all compelling factors dismissed by a score. This numeric judgment opens and closes doors to teachers, schools, lessons, friends, jobs, homes, neighborhoods, lives, and future lives. Presently, these numbers are influencing the very nature of school in this country. Numbers are often manipulated by agenda? Consequently, I chose to research qualitatively in a conscious effort to invite and reveal the human experience. This study is reliant upon the candor and genius of its subjects, not upon information tallied from scoreboards and ledgers.

CHAPTER FOUR

●

RICK MALNATI:
NEW TRIER AND FENWICK HIGH SCHOOLS

"The key is always teamwork"

"Here We Come! Here We Come!" the Trevian faithful clad in blue, green, and white raucously chanted while bouncing in unison, Duke University style, on the rickety bleachers of venerable Gates Gymnasium prior to the opening tip. The New Trier fan base was remarkable. Unified students armed with clever invectives and electrified by expectation, older folks, parents, families, faculty, administration, and most notably alumni are ever present. Why did Trevian basketball command such a loyal following? A tradition of excellence, wholesome entertainment, and community support were all probable reasons, but New Trier loyalty ran deep and that crazed Italian conductor on the sidelines, exhorting his players to harmoniously overachieve, stoked the fire of Trevian loyalty as intensely as any coach ever has. "Leaders are the architects of improved individual and organizational performance." (Reeves)

Rick Malnati cared about family. His former players actively contributed to the Trevian family; many coached and scouted voluntarily. He invited them back to speak to his current team and bridge the future with the storied past. These former players were proud of their connection with Rick. They glowed when they were able to report an insight into Rick's mindset or a new wrinkle in the Trevian attack. Rick was one of those people always on the move in search of a better way or a more interesting challenge. People were drawn to his fiery passion for life and his insatiable search for his next cause. He created a strong belief system that binds the work of its constituents into "a coherent set of actions. Like most other belief systems, this one is not written down, but is expressed in the words and actions of people in the system." (Darling-Hammonds)

How I Met Rick Malnati

During my first year as head coach at Evanston High School, weeks prior to the New Trier game, I began to understand just how important victory over the Trevians was, not only for our excitable students and faithful fans, but for faculty, coaches, administration, and the city of Evanston as well. My assistants who bled orange and blue for most of their lives hated Rick Malnati. They perceived him as arrogant, manipulative, and perhaps most offensively, a product of the Winnetka community. We, the self-proclaimed blue-collar types from Evanston, fanned the emotional flames already ablaze from the 100-year rivalry into some kind of class war. Malnati, the Pizza King, represented the rich, elitist, cake eaters to the north. By the grace of divine intervention, we upset the heavily favored Trevians that December evening, but more important than the victory, Rick and I were thrust into a friendship that neither of us knew at the time was probable. Weeks prior to the game, I scouted the Trevs and their warrior coach. I learned quickly how passionate Rick was about precision, urgency, selflessness, and honor. Rick Malnati was tortured by the notion of imperfection. He was painfully intolerant of inefficiency and violently intolerant of a lack of effort. His teams comported themselves with exceptional poise and savvy. They spread the floor, saw opportunity, and struck when their dominant fitness wore down defensive opponents.

New Trier motion offense used every square inch of the floor and involved long fast cuts, bruising blind screens, and head-spinning ball movement. Rick conducted this symphony by stomping his right foot and exhorting his troops with his ear-piercing voice and his expressive nose-crinkled scowl. Like a wounded animal empowered by pain and adrenalin, the extra gear that he engaged as a scrappy player taking on the world was alive and well in his coaching persona. He was Bruce Springsteen meets Jake Lamotta. One would be hard pressed to find a coach who intensely plans, prepares, demands, and executes at a level any higher than Rick Malnati. His being was raw, honest, and relentless; his pursuit of perfection insatiable.

"Try not to become a man of success,
but rather try to become a man of value."

~Albert Einstein

Why would a partner of one of the most successful restaurant chains in America, Lou Malnati's Pizza, choose to leave his role to pursue a degree in education with the hope of becoming a high school teacher and basketball coach? This thought process epitomized the drive within Rick Malnati. His maniacal quest was fueled by fear, anger, and, like Albert Einstein, an intense desire to bring value to the world.

The Conversation

His physical education colleagues long gone for the weekend, Coach Rick Malnati sat alone in his cramped office enjoying the chilly Lake Michigan breeze that invigorated his work place. Stacks of paper, plans, recordings, practice gear, files, and oddly, trophies; scores of trophies adorned every available space in his 8'x 8' office that he shared with New Trier baseball coach Mike Napolean. Regional and even Sectional Championship plaques, revered as gold in most schools, garnered little respect at vaunted New Trier High School. The pressure to succeed at such a prestigious institution must have been overwhelming for teachers and coaches, let alone students, and was evidenced by these quarantined symbols of excellence. The chaotic intensity of Rick's office reeked of genius and industry, with a hint of eccentricity.

He immediately asked about my family, my work, and me…not just to ask, but his follow-ups revealed his genuine curiosity about my life. He listened like an adventurer seeking new ideas. Additionally, he wanted to know if I was well. This quality, concern for those in his life, defined Rick Malnati. Realizing that he had reversed our roles, I promptly regained my interviewer status. He proceeded to tell his remarkable story, warts and all, partly because he is bluntly non-pretentious and partly because he wanted me to succeed in writing my dissertation. How fortunate his players must have been to have this generous force of nature in their lives.

He proclaimed that his intensity was derived through fear and anger and that both of these factors evolved during his tumultuous childhood. Rick's father came to America in 1948. Lou Malnati was an 18-year-old Italian immigrant looking to make his mark in the volatile restaurant industry. After many years working, learning, and carousing with the folks at Pizzeria Uno and Due in downtown Chicago, Lou took his recipe and opened Lou Malnati's Pizza restaurants in Lincolnwood and Elk Grove Village in Illinois. Long hours often punctuated by heavy drinking stole time and focus from Lou's family life. Lou was boorish at times. As a young boy, concerned for the safety of his mother, Rick carefully designed a plan to stop his father if Lou's three o'clock in the morning abusive fits of rage ever crossed the line.

At the time of this study, Rick still harbored intense anger toward his father who died when Rick was just 18; but if you cut through the layers of emotional scarring, there was a strong argument that the demanding brutality of Lou Malnati may very well have been the incendiary that lit Rick Malnati with such fiery illumination.

Our conversation turned to many subjects: Rick's wife Tina and their children, his faith in God, playing career, business career, decision to pursue education, program philosophy, former players and staff members, mentors, and countless others. As Rick revealed his story, it profoundly clarified why he had evolved into such a charismatic force on the court. His hunger for his father's approval triggered emotion fueled by fear and anger that exploded into unabashed competitive energy. *Winning* earned Rick Malnati respect.

Early Years: Wilmette, Illinois

Rick Joseph Malnati and his older brother Marc grew up in Wilmette, Illinois. Like other Chicago North Shore suburbs, the Wilmette community took great pride in its schools, parks, and tree-lined avenues. Because Rick's family invested most of their time and resources into the pizzeria business and Rick was too young to contribute, he often found himself alone. This alone time was consumed by athletics. He gravitated to basketball because it was available in his driveway, he didn't need others to play, and it provided him with a vehicle to improve his skills. Rick enjoyed the reflective nature of shooting hoops all hours of the day and night and the escape that it gave him. Like most junior high kids, Rick struggled with identity. Schoolwork didn't interest him and his family fought hard to build the business, which left little time for affirmation. Rick found identity through sports. When Marc wasn't working at the restaurant, he would include Rick in various neighborhood contests. Rick grew up fast, competing against athletes three and four years older than he. This athletic apprenticeship led to prominence in the Park District and school-organized baseball and basketball leagues. It also inspired his father Lou to take notice of Rick's achievements.

Despite his disdain for his father's bullying, Rick vied for Lou's approval saying: "To get my father's approval, I needed to win." Lou would often pit his sons Rick and Marc against each other. Marc the better student and Rick the better athlete created tension and discomfort for both. When Lou attended Rick's Little League games, Rick would do his level best to succeed in order to entice his father to come again. Once Rick had established himself as a standout performer, Lou seemed to revel in his son's success.

In March of 1978, Lou Malnati succumbed to the cancer that had plagued him for six years. Rick's tumultuous relationship with his proud father physically ended that evening, but continued to drive Rick's intensity, which was still present at the time of my interview with him.

In high school, Rick accepted his first major athletic mission, lifting New Trier West High School to its first regional championship over New Trier East in the school's history:

> I was sitting on the bench at the end of the game. Winning
> that game was my biggest sports accomplishment. Even
> though we won the sectional and the super sectional that year,

it was winning the regional that was special because we did
something everybody said we could not do. (Rick)

Malnati thrived on achieving the improbable. Planning, scheming, and
strategizing were methods he employed even as a high school student. Rick
described his attempts to plant seeds of doubt in the mind of Coach John
Schneiter, the lauded coach of perennial powerhouse and nemesis New
Trier East:

> I knew John Schneiter would be running at the track over at
> New Trier West. I would go out at night and I would sprint
> on the football field as he'd be running, consciously. I'd get
> worn out. He didn't really talk to me and I didn't talk to him,
> but I knew him and he was kind of like the God around here.
> He was very successful. I'd bring some teammates out once
> in a while and we'd run in front of him, just to let him know
> we were not like the past NTW teams. We wound up beating
> them three times in my senior year. (Rick)

Whether his tactic to unnerve Coach Schneiter worked is to be debated,
but Rick's approach to gamesmanship was rife with examples of the art of subtle
seed planting.

As Rick excelled through high school, his relationship with his dad
improved. Lou took great pride in his son's athletic prowess and became one
of the New Trier West Cowboys' most ardent fans. As Lou's cancer escalated,
he was unable to witness the Cowboys' run to the State Championship, but
engineered a deal for the games to be broadcast on local radio through the
sponsorship of Lou Malnati's Pizza.

"I'll bring the energy. I'm the energy guy," stated Rick about his role as a
standout player at New Trier West and then at Bradley University. "I have a
gear fueled by fear and anger that most players don't have." The heat of that gear
is rarely comfortable. His own teammates caught the brunt of Rick's intensity
when he demanded their best effort, and more than one official was pushed

to assess a technical foul on young Rick. Those who competed against Rick understood that he possessed an ability to "will" his teams to victory. That same gear that he exercised as a player was the foundation for his success as a teacher and coach. It would be difficult to find an educator better prepared, more passionate, or more able to articulate his vision.

Malnati Mentors: Goran, Sheets, and Stowell
Coach John Goran

Among the many coaching mentors throughout Rick's life, three seemed to have special prominence: John Goran, Ricks' PE teacher in grade school; the venerable Trevian coach Mel Sheets; and Joe Stowell, Rick's first head coach at Bradley University. Rick spoke fondly of them all:

> My favorite guy growing up was my grade school PE Coach Goran. He was just a big, strong guy. The fact that he would say good things about me and use me as an example with other kids, made me feel proud. I learned about the different intelligences and I was physically intelligent and he praised that. So I learned self-esteem, I think. I learned feeling good about myself at a time when I didn't feel good about myself. Everywhere else in school was a scary place and my refuge was in the gym. He made things a big deal. He kept stats in IM sports. He would keep these things and he'd make a Field Day that was unbelievable. In fact, I want to have a Field Day at New Trier because it was such a great memory. He made it so important. I'm a PE teacher now somewhat because of him. He had a big influence on me. (Rick)

Coach Goran enkindled the prospects for leadership in young Malnati. Rick became fascinated with the influence leaders have in the lives of people and the systems to which they are connected. Sergiovanni noted:

> Leaders care deeply about the people in the system. They want the system to be successful. They want the system to make a

respected contribution to society. They want the system to contribute to the quality of life of people who are involved in it.

Coach Mel Sheets

Young Malnati challenged his coaches. Fortunately, Mel Sheets saw beyond Rick's cantankerous demeanor and patiently guided him toward success:

> Although Coach Sheets became much more of a mentor later on in my life, I learned from him in high school. When I was going into senior year at NTW, there were two grads that were going to be freshman in college that were playing this one-on-one game and they were on the main court. And they kept playing, but we were ready to scrimmage. Sheets says, "Let them play." I said, "What do you mean let them play? Get them off. Get them off the court."
>
> He said, "Just let them play. Why are you so upset?" I said, "What do you mean, why am I so upset? You know I like these guys, but get them off the frickin' floor. It's time for us to play." And he kept on in his southern drawl: "Let 'em play. Why are you like that?" I said, screw that. So, I left. I left and I quit the basketball team for a few weeks in the summer.
>
> My parents were out of town. My grandparents stayed with me. We had a summer league game at Deerfield. I didn't go to the summer league game. I didn't go back to New Trier West all week. This is my team, my guys, and all my friends. I said, screw that. I am not going back. I'm going to transfer to New Trier East. New Trier East, to me, they were the guys who played hard and always beat us. So I admit I was hard to coach. I'm sure he hasn't had many guys like me. So a week later, my mom and dad came home. I said: "Hey, I want to go to New Trier East." My dad said: "You can't go to New Trier East.

You've got to live in the district. You can't just go to New Trier
East." I told him what happened. He said: "You had better go in
there and apologize." "I'm not going to apologize. He didn't get
my story. I was so right. How could you not understand how
right I am?" He was like: "You're a baby." I said: "I'm not going
back. I'm quittin'." He said: "You've got to go back." So I go
back the next day and go to my locker to get my stuff. Coach
Sheets said in his southern drawl: "Oh, you're back." I was like
screw you. It would just fuel me. I hated that. He didn't show
any emotion. I thought whatever, and just went upstairs to the
gym and practiced. (Rick)

Mel Sheets was a veteran coach. He had seen it all during his long and
successful career. He understood that self-actualization will only occur if the
subject is allowed the freedom to grow, stretch, challenge, and often, fail.

One thing I'll say about him is he gave me as a player a lot of
say. We'd be in the huddle and he'd ask what play did *I* want and
the guys believed in me. He allowed me freedom. I could make
mistakes and I would never come out. I'm not sure I could
coach me. You know? He allowed me space to be me and make
mistakes with the thought that there is something good going
to happen. I lose sight of that sometimes when I coach my
players. He gave me space to be me. He didn't have to control
everything to feel comfortable. He was okay with himself. He
felt confident in himself enough that he let me be me. (Rick)

Coach Sheets' role in the development of Rick's teaching style harkens
the work of Goleman on Emotional Intelligence as well as the celebration of
individuals' talents. Rick realized he was difficult to coach. Many exceptional
players are. Coach Sheets taught Rick the value of freeing players to become
their best. The Trevians under Malnati operated with supreme confidence
emanating from their collective sense of freedom.

Coach Joe Stowell

Malnati was recruited and mentored by Joe Stowell at Bradley University in Peoria, Illinois. Again, Rick encountered a calm, patient, and deliberate coach who modeled respect and community building:

> And then in college, Coach Stowell, who is just a great guy. His recruitment of me was not…it wasn't like there was a war to get me. At Christmastime (freshman year at Bradley), we had a chance to go to Spain. Out of the 12 guys on the team, he was only taking 10, could only afford 10. So every time he said you're one of the 10 guys, I said: "Well, I don't want to go. I'll just go home and spend time with my dad." He said: "Is he dying?" I said: "Yeah." He had cancer. He had it in his lung, his head, his eyes…Coach really respected that. His dad was an alcoholic. There were a lot of parallels.

> Later in the season my mom called Coach Stowell to tell me my dad was dying and to get me home right away. So, next thing I know…he was in my room saying: "You've got a flight at 6:00 in the morning. There's going to be somebody to pick you up at the airport. Your dad's not doing well."

> So I leave and go home. They denied dad pain medication to delay his death until I could say goodbye. As soon as I got there, I talked to him a little bit and then they gave him the medicine to make him slow down and take the pain away. He died an hour later. He was 48—my age right now. He was at Northwestern Memorial. There is a plaque on the cancer ward floor and that's from my family's work with the Lou Malnati cancer dinner we have every year in his honor.

> The services were Saturday and Monday. We started the Missouri Valley Conference on that Tuesday. Coach Stowell

drives all the way up to the service on Monday, stays 15 minutes at the service just to say hi and leaves. He missed Monday's practice to come to my dad's funeral and missed, potentially, his last practice ever (he knew Bradley would dismiss him after the season) and I was a guy who never played. We wound up winning that next game and played again two nights later, but Coach Stowell was willing to miss his last practice ever at BU to come to my dad's funeral. It was like, wow, for me he came and did that for me. That was kind of a great model for me of what you should do for the kids you coach. That was beyond the call of duty. I'll always remember that. It was the right thing for him to do. (Rick)

Coach Stowell recognized the value of relationship building. His actions were genuine and from the heart. He possessed a basic fundamental respect for the wellbeing of those around him. His humanity reminds me of the commitment that Rick and another well-known coach from Chicago shared with their players. Coach Krzyzewski explained this in his own words:

I've been forming teams since I was a kid in Chicago. It's what I enjoy most in life. It's what I do. Almost everything in leadership comes back to relationships. And, naturally, the level of cooperation on any team increases tremendously as the level of trust rises. The only way you can possibly lead people is to understand people. And the best way to understand them is to get to know them better.

Becoming a Coach: "It Wasn't My Dream to be a Pizza Guy"

After college, Rick joined his brother Marc and his mother Jean in the family business. They added a carryout store in Wilmette and Marc asked Rick to help organize the kitchens in all the stores to improve efficiency. Rick enjoyed the collaboration, pace, and heat of the kitchen. He entered each store as a teammate, but because of his family name the staff deferred to him. Rick instilled "sports model" practices to build better kitchens. The staff responded and during this time the Malnati restaurant business began its boldest expansion—new sites, new menu items, new catering initiatives, and the introduction of "Lou To Go." As the Malnati juggernaut became a multi-million dollar business, Rick was frequently reminded of his athletic journey and was particularly perplexed by the vast divide between the suburban wealthy and urban poor. His Bradley University experience exposed him to teammates who became brothers, but had it not been for the common ground of basketball, the kid from Wilmette would never have met the kids from the West Side of Chicago. At the same time in 1986, Rick connected to the Fellowship for Christian Athletes (FCA) and envisioned a time when he could purchase a site and facility and develop a camp that would provide suburban and urban kids a place to break down barriers of race, stereotype, and class through the commonality of basketball. In order for this vision to be realized, Rick recognized that he needed to realign himself in the high school hoops milieu and sought the counsel of his friend and mentor Coach Mel Sheets.

I included the preceding paragraph to underscore Rick's life experiences that helped to formulate his ambitious approach to teaching. He was a natural leader in the Malnati kitchens and business deals. Rick brought that same leadership, organization, and passion back to the classrooms of New Trier and built a vision inspired by the possibility of building an alliance through the FCA:

> I went back to Coach Sheets and I said: "Hey, I need to take orders from somebody. I just need to know if I can handle that discipline. I want to know if I can do that. It was kind of a self-discipline thing. Would you consider me working with you?" And he said: "Oh, yeah. I'll give you the sophomore team." I said: "No, no. I don't want my own team. I don't want to have to be the head coach. I want to work with you. I want to be an assistant coach to you." So, then I was able to work for him, which was good. It was a good self-discipline thing to see if I could be a good employee. And I wasn't that good of

an employee; I wanted to do a lot of things differently. Coach gave me a lot of responsibility and allowed me to have a voice in almost everything we were doing.

But, then it came to the point where I was doing this youth group, the FCA group, and I was really involved in church and my relationship with God and everything. I was just getting pushed that this is what I should be doing. I'm good at this and I could build relationships with kids in the suburbs and hopefully connect them with kids in the city. That was my experience in college. I grew up in the suburbs and never knew people that much different than me even though I was pretty much different from a lot of the people I grew up with being first generation Italian, but I never felt different. Knowing that kids are kids, and trying to bridge that gap, I was doing that as an assistant coach with Wolf Nelson at Farragut Public High School in Chicago. We'd do this FCA and I felt like I was just getting prodded by God and I've got to do this. My goal was to be successful enough and build relationships that I would have a camp that would connect city and suburban kids and it's a regret that I haven't followed through on that. (Rick)

Rick flourished under the guidance of Coach Sheets and quickly won the confidence of the players as he devised defensive drills, schemes, and philosophy to complement the Trevian system. When Coach Sheets began to ponder retirement, athletic director Bob Naughton invited Rick to consider the post. However, the head coach was required to be a certified teacher and Rick did not have the proper credentials. The best of both worlds—business by day and hoops hobby at night—was about to change. Rick quickly enrolled in school full-time, continued to work full-time, and coached even more intensely than ever while helping his then fiancée, Tina, cope with her ailing mother. If it weren't for the support of his brother Marc, he would have backed away from the notion of being a head coach.

After an exhausting national search, Rick Malnati was named head coach at New Trier High School in the spring of 1996. He completed his degree in education, joined the faculty, and with the help of Wolf Nelson of Farragut High School continued to engage suburban and urban players through various means.

The Strength of the Wolf is in the Pack

The art of teaching, according to Rick Malnati, is founded in creating an environment that stirs players to grow together. Rick said, "It's important that we spend a lot of time together; there's a lot of passion when we spend time together because we become invested in each other." Time was critical to the Trevians. School ended at 3:25 p.m. Players were expected to be shooting by 3:30 p.m. and loose for practice by 3:40 p.m.:

> I hate the jacking around. Some coaches might say the jacking around is good for them; but no, I want two guys at a basket shooting. I mean, you can talk, but they better be shooting, you know, I don't want the grab-ass. I want them focused. I mean, hey, this is my time now. We're going now. (Rick)

Practices were comprised of carefully designed segments of time. Rick tried to follow the practice plan, but admitted, "We'll go over it sometimes until the cows come home. We'll go till it's done right."

As November approached, Rick reviewed practice plans from past campaigns and tailored them to complement his new squad:

> I'm much more prepared at the beginning of the year. I have everything written out so all of the coaches know what's going on, and it winds up pretty much at the beginning of the year, you know with tryouts and everything, we're doing pretty much the same thing. You know, this year (2007–2008) we have nine returning guys so they should hit the floor running more. Especially as far as what we were doing, and growing on what we did. Sometimes you've got to start, you know, are

they on breast milk or are they on solid foods? Where are
they as a team; what can they handle? But we'll practice the
first week...we'll have twelve practices in by Sunday, that first
day off, because we'll go before school and after school. Even
in January, December...we had the kids come in a couple of
mornings just to shoot. They think they get out earlier by
coming in and shooting, but the more they shoot...they shoot
well. We'll run a lot of good plays; but if you can't shoot it in at
the end of the play, then you might as well count on losing...
so we'll do a lot of shooting. I have a coach this year coming
before school two days a week to just do shooting. So, he's
going to be working Mondays and Wednesdays before school
shooting and that's going to be his role besides watching films
with me, but he's not going to come to practice after practice
Monday/Wednesday. It works better for his family; it works
better for us. (Rick)

The inevitability of change and all of its complexity permeates basketball
programs. Rick accepted and maximized the opportunities that change
presented to his organization. He would agree that, "although change is
unpredictable, you can set up conditions that help to guide the process." (Fullan)

Malnati coached teams to play to their strengths, often emphasizing
new concepts, but holding fast to the tried and true staples that defined New
Trier basketball:

I hate the weekend before my first practice in November. What
am I going to do in the first practice? If you go in this file, I'll
have my practices from every year. I'll take five books out and
I'll look back at my first day of practice every year. I say: "What
am I doing?" Somebody just needs to kick me in the face and
say: "Rick, you can do this in your sleep. Now, be prepared,
but this is what you do." Finally, I'm at the point where I don't
need it all perfectly written. Just get your thoughts down, get

your vision set, write it down and be organized; there's going to be a flaw but that's not my strength. My strength is not in the organizational part. I heard somebody say they charted everything they were going to do all summer before summer started. Football teams do that or something. They have everything planned. That is not me. Although it's attractive, it's like if you do that it's unbelievable. You are so smart. You do it that way; I'm going to do it my way. I think now I've got the confidence to say that and not get trapped in the thinking I'm not good enough. (Rick)

Practice Makes Permanent

The Trevians balanced an inside out attack because year in and year out they shot from the perimeter with laser-like accuracy. Rick explained his approach to teaching the art of shooting. He also demonstrated his natural talent for prioritization and the emphasis on simple, measurable, and attainable goal setting:

There's a picture…a Marquette picture where a kid's penetrating the lane and there's four guys on the perimeter all down ready to catch. Every time, you should be down ready to catch. Any time there's penetration. They probably have this picture in their minds of shooting, you know, foot back and hands ready…delivering the ball, just making good passes off of penetration, having pride in your pass. They'll make some bad passes and I'll say something to them like "we're not livin' like this…it's not okay. Either you switch jerseys or we're running or something." There are certain things as a coach you really work at and focus on. For me that would be shooting and the preparation to shoot. You know, if they don't get an offensive rebound for eight minutes in a quarter, I don't even realize it because that's not a thing we work a lot on. But, on our team, if they're not ready to catch the ball or if they throw the ball away, it's heightened because that's something we try to be really good at. So we practice shooting a lot and people who watch us practice say you know you spend a lot of time shooting. Yeah, we do. (Rick)

Another perennial characteristic of Trevian players was their collective physical toughness. Few teams defended, blocked out, took the charge, and dived for loose balls at a rate comparable to New Trier. Rick described the delicate balance between conditioning and potential injury:

We practice two times a day for the first week of the season. Our kids are in the gym the first Monday at 5:30 a.m. We don't baby them. They get hurt, but it's a mental toughness that you cannot teach, you know. They're champing at the bit early in the year. So, I know kids get tired after the first couple of days. My first year, after about seven kids suffered minor inconvenient injuries, the trainer came and said, "Rick, what are you doing?" right in front of the team. I said "don't ever talk to me like that again in front of my team. Don't ever say that again. I know what I'm doing." You always run the risk of injury. You don't want the kids run down, but I think they look forward to it. As much as they complain, there's a badge of honor and that badge of honor is important. They know they've got to run a 5:30 mile; they know and it's like "We did it; we accomplished it!" You need that stuff in your soul when you're going up to the free throw line (late in a game). I want them to be in better shape by the end of the year, but I want them to come to me in the best shape they've ever been in their life. And, I think that's a good goal. (Rick)

So much of coaching this marathon of a season requires vision reliant on experience. Malnati recognized the breathing and pace of a basketball season and was exceptionally equipped to look ahead to the future. He was willing to take one step back today for two steps forward in the future. "A good leader has to look beyond what his team is doing now—or there could be serious consequences down the road. Whatever a leader does now sets up what he does later. And there's always a later." (Krzyzewski).

Life Balance: What Do You Win When You Win?

Malnati admitted that the combination of all factors underscored by the pressure of winning haunted him:

> Sadly enough I could really get caught up in the wins and the losses and feeling that pressure where we've got to do better every year and it's never good enough. I just got caught up in that and I got away from my original vision of why I wanted to do this. (Rick)

Rick acknowledged how fortunate he was to share life with his understanding and patient wife, Tina, and their thriving children, but he was not proud of his need to isolate after a tough loss, or his inability to be physically and emotionally present at times during the seasons. "It's a sad state of affairs, but sometimes I'm a better coach for my basketball team than I am at home. I'm more effective with my basketball team."

He joked about winter holidays with his extended family and their travel plans to warmer climates while he was preoccupied with the preparation for foes at the Proviso West Holiday Tournament in "balmy" Hillside, Illinois. Staying healthy was challenging during the 18-week grind of the season:

> I'll be prepared mentally, but physically I don't do a great job of staying healthy. You know, I go one-dimensional during basketball. Last night I was up at five in the morning thinking about basketball. I'm an adrenaline junkie. I'm not an alcoholic, but adrenaline…I'm addicted to that, you know. Even though I don't like it, I'll get myself in that position somehow because it is what's normal to me. It's what's normal; it's what's comfortable. Somehow I'm hard-wired like that. I like the

feeling of adrenaline. If I'm not doing something competitive with basketball, I will dream about gambling; I just want to go to the boat. Now, I don't go to the boat that often, but I think about it a lot, just because that is the same kind of rush. That's why I like good movies or books during the season also. I need distractions; otherwise, all I think about is basketball. I'm a "sicko"! (Rick)

When Rick described his love of battling in the competitive theater; he revealed why he chose to compromise quality of life elsewhere:

I try and play floor hockey with guys at New Trier, you know, I tried to play basketball last week. And, I love that and I need that because otherwise where do I get that (rush)? Where am I going to get that if I stop coaching? I'll be...Friday, wake up for a game, you know, first game...whatever, or two days before I'll start getting a little nervous...and then before the game. I've kind of got a thing that I do where I want to be really clear-headed for the game. I want to remember everything that I've done to prepare myself. I want to read through my notes; I want to take a nap when I get home when it's game day. My wife knows when it's game day, tell the kids it's game day, you know, stay away from dad right now! I am just so focused in. I'm hyper-vigilant to the point where I can't enjoy friends that I see before the game. I'm rude, but I'm not trying to be rude. It's just like that's how I always competed, you know, I wasn't one of those guys who was "hey, how are ya?" I was always, kind of, this is the game and this is so important for me that I'm focusing everything I have on it. I've got to win! It's all about winning. That's how you get your self-esteem, you know; for me, I was important and I was okay if I won. So, I carry that on. That's the bad part of competition for me. That's the part that makes me not want to do this. I'm trying to change and I did a good job last year being more invested in my family…more aware of what's going on. But, otherwise, during the season and Christmas, I have a game at Proviso the 26th. I can't even enjoy watching the kids opening gifts; I'm just worried that I've got to play Fenwick or I've got to play St. Joe tomorrow…I was going to try and celebrate them [holidays] in August! (Rick)

Those closest to Rick, especially Tina, worried about his intensity:

My wife is repulsed sometimes when she hears what I may have said to one of my players. I understand her concern and disappointment. I'm not proud of this part of me, what I say at times; but I have relationships I have built with most of my guys and they know I care about them. (Rick)

He was cognizant of the opinion that some feel he may be too passionate for the good of the players and himself, but Rick counters:

It frustrates me. Those kids are probably much more balanced and grounded than I was or still am about winning and losing. They are much healthier. I tell them: "Guys, I'm off balance on this, I've got to tell you. But if you want to win, it's available to you, but this is what you've got to do to get there." Thankfully my kids, they'll be pretty disciplined. They grow up disciplined, but they didn't grow up as aggressive. My job is to get them to be both. When people watch me stomp on the ground, they may think I'm really obnoxious. I have fun, though, you know. I'm free, you know; when I'm out there, I'm free. I don't care what you think and I don't care what anybody thinks of me and that's a nice way to live. (Rick)

Rick Malnati was ultra-reflective. He constantly evaluated his contribution to the world, his strengths and shortcomings, his relationships with those he loves, and his understanding of God all in the vein of becoming a better human being. He admitted his complex persona stirs anxiety:

> My hard-wiring, my family dynamics, you know, whatever it is…I'm ultra-responsible in some stuff. I feel ultra-responsible for…like my brother's a spender and I'm a saver. If he spends too much, then I am the responsible one who's got to bail him out because I've saved all of the time, yet he's living and I'm saving. But, that's how I do things. I save; I prepare. I wish I wasn't like that, you know; I wish I was different, but those are the battles that I have to fight. That's how I am. I'm like a "depression baby" but I'm not like that with food. I can waste with the best of them when it comes to wasting. I'm always worried about what could happen that probably will never happen. Sometimes that's haunting in a way. It's not the way you want to live, you know; I'd rather live just thinking all the best thoughts, but that's what comes natural to me is to think of what if this; what if that. I then relate that to basketball. I prepare. I know that I can over-prepare and some teams just don't do great with that much information, and I'm like, "What the hell am I doing?" I should be spending my time on other things, worried about us more than them. (Rick)

Even if I knew how tortured Rick was within his own thought process, I would have been unable to take advantage of this insight when I prepared to compete against the Trevians. Malnati was obsessive about various aspects of preparation, but therein laid his genius. His inner conflicts defined his approach, and his approach was extraordinary. As agonizing as it must have been to live in Rick's skin, the end product was often glorious, further complicating his personal dilemma. His perfection was Beethoven-like, as captured in the 1994 film *Immortal Beloved.*

Philosophy: Urgency and Honesty

The Malnati approach to teaching, coaching, and living one's life is summarized in two concepts: urgency and honesty. Rick believed his players needed to know where they stood, what their roles were, and how they could improve their value to the team. Periodic meetings occurred throughout the season, but Rick carefully tended to each of his players when he conducted individual pre-season meetings. In these meetings, he learned about each player's aspirations and unveiled his expectations for each player as well. He urged them to be true to their innate gifts, and relished awards night each season when he publicly articulated his admiration for each of his Trevians, particularly his seniors. This presence in his players' lives was especially valuable at a time in American culture when adolescents on average spent less than five percent of available time with their parents. Rick reflected on this:

> This is their Bar Mitzvah. Did you ever go to a Bar Mitzvah and hear the parents talk about their kids? I cry just hearing the parents talk about their kids, giving them a vision, giving them this speech. What a gift. It's like giving them a blessing. And sometimes I tell kids stuff that they don't want to hear, but it's honest; I think it's truthful. I know them. I know them sometimes better than their parents know them. I've been with them two years. (Rick)

The Role of Strategy: So Much More than Xs and Os

Malnati manipulated factors that contribute to basketball excellence as well as any coach. However, he acknowledged that technical acumen, X's and O's, represent a minimal part in coaching:

> When I go to round tables [brainstorming idea exchanges] and guys are talking basketball, I think they are talking sometimes in a language that I never learned. They're talking about the single side, the double side, this cut, that cut, and I'm like holy cow they just know way more. Where do they teach this class? Maybe because I haven't played in a long time, I think I've

gotten to the point where my job is to be a master motivator, to just motivate my kids and make them believe in things that they don't believe in. Like vision, give them a vision, cast a vision and stay true to that vision. The X's and O's, they're important, but getting kids to play together and play the right way is essential.

There is a flow within the game and within the players where they are kind of lost in the game. It's like they don't even have to think. It just [snaps his fingers], they are going to places that they go just on instinct. There could be 1,000 people or 5,000 or nobody and it wouldn't matter much. Somehow they feel that the good parts of human nature are all behind them. It's like I'm playing and everybody that loves me, not only are they at the game, but they want me to be successful. And there is not much downside if I'm not successful. You just feel weightless. It's just like you're in a flow. You are just lost. And that's the thing I like about sports. (Rick)

Goal Setting: High Achievement Follows High Expectation

When developing its season's schedule, New Trier like all schools attempted to provide a challenging and enjoyable experience for its student athletes. The selection of opponents, tournaments, and venues is a critical element in the health of the program. Not surprisingly, Malnati's Trevians sought the very best in competition. Some coaches pepper their schedules with "cupcakes," not Rick. Preparing next season's schedule of opponents is much like designing the level of curricular rigor for a classroom teacher. Over or underestimate the talent level of your students, and the learning experience can become unnecessarily frustrating:

And so it's like when I'm scheduling, oh, is this going to be fun! I'm looking at the schedule. Look at these teams! This is awesome! And my kids are liking it when I'm talking about it, but then when they're actually living it, they are just fatigued. Usually at the end of the year, at the last week of the year, we'll barely beat somebody for a conference championship or we'll lose to somebody we shouldn't lose to because my kids are emotionally frickin' drained and I am too.

I think that it would be smarter on one hand to not have a tough schedule because a lot of coaches seed teams for the state tournament on record. But I like the results that are provided and the fact that when you play a top ten team and you've already faced a team like that, there are no surprises, and your ultimate goal is to advance through the state tournament. Our goals aren't much during the season. Let's play the championship game. Let's play the last day of every tournament we play in. So if we play and beat Evanston twice, that's a goal usually. Just talking about those days of the wins and the losses are a roller coaster. The games we schedule are going to be memories for the kids. The more that you ask of your kids or yourself, the more you give. (Rick)

Coach Malnati continued to express his obsession with control when articulating his perspective about team defense:

I am motivated a lot by fear and fear is not a great motivator. I'm motivated by not being embarrassed...by not being humiliated; so when it comes to game preparation, I'm always looking at my angle. I would say I'm a defensive coach first.... I make my adjustments more defensively; that's how I see the game of basketball. Some guys are offensive guys; some guys are defensive guys. I sub defensively, but when I watch another team, I always see what they could do to expose us. You know, like. "Wow man, they're going to kill us!" As game week comes up my kids would say I over-sell the other team a lot of the time. And, uh, sometimes that's okay, a good thing; sometimes that's a bad thing. The better the team, the less I over-sell them; but I think my kids know me and know who we're playing. The motivation is to not be humiliated, and not lose to a team that we should beat, and not be embarrassed by a team that's better than us. What you do is out in the public and everybody gets a chance to look at your finished product, and it's scary. I'm counting on sixteen-, seventeen-, and eighteen-year-old kids to represent themselves, but also represent me. It's like I'm leading an orchestra or something and I want the orchestra to sound right. Even though I'm not playing an instrument, I'm the guy who got them to mesh together. (Rick)

Inevitability of Change: Journey, Not Destination

As a conductor, Rick annually selected arrangements that accentuate the talents of his musicians:

I plan a year ahead. Bob Williams, one of the guy's I most respect at Schaumburg…he'll play the same way with no matter who he has. That's just the Schaumburg way. That's Bob's way. I play differently…you know; there might be two or three years we play the same way. But, we're playing more like when I first got the job, now. I'm a man-to-man guy; I'd much rather play man-to man. I love the pressure; I love to play like that. I have more control. I have the control then. I can't do that with my team this year. I'm going to have to be a one-three-one guy, a two-three, a match-up zone, you know, two-two-one, full court, pick your traps; be smart. Get kids to understand what we really do well and what we really do poorly. Well, fun is winning. Fun ain't going out and playing Marshall up and down and losing 100 to 70. As a coach, your job is to give your team the best chance to win, right? (Rick)

With regard to concepts he valued most in his players, Rick spoke of passion, confidence, teamwork, and investment:

> You know, to have passion for something. The whole goal at the end of the year is…how did we develop as a team? Like, were we always thinking about me, me, and me or was each player worried about his team and having fun with his teammates…being honest with his teammates and going for something that's bigger than you. You know, like risking and taking big risks and having big goals…maybe falling on your face, but still going for it. So, I think I want them to learn; I don't know if you learn confidence, but to have confidence and to accomplish things that if they thought to themselves beforehand "Aw, we can't do that" and they actually were able to do it. You know, it's like, use that as a part of them that they keep with them forever and can say, "I remember when we did this or I did this.… " You know, some personal accomplishment that they're able to keep in their soul.
>
> And, some of the teams we've had might not have been some of the greatest teams, but knowing when you're on a good team…what it looks like, what it feels like, what it tastes like, and then duplicate that in their business and in their families. To just strive for…knowing that there's something good out there and striving for it and not just settling. But living with a little passion…just going for it! And, if they're able to perform in the games that they play in, and under the pressure they're under, they've got a pretty good chance of doin' it. They play in some pretty big games, in front of a lot of people. They've got a lot at stake…a lot at risk. They've worked hard enough and invested enough, so that if they lose, it's a big loss. If you don't invest much and you lose, it's no big deal, right? But, if you invest a lot and you lose, it's like, "Oh, my God, why did I

do that!" You either feel like an idiot, or it's like, it was worth it.
Even though I lost, it was worth it. (Rick)

Malnati echoed the words of Thoreau, "and not, when I came to die, discover that I have not lived." In summary, Rick continued to summon the tenets of transcendentalism when he revealed:

> I think the one thing that's worked is being true to who I am.
> I tried at the beginning of my head coaching career to be like
> Lon Krueger on the sidelines the first three games…just cool
> and calm, but it just wasn't me. So, the next time we're playing
> Deerfield who's ranked fourth and we're zero and three and
> I was me and we played a lot better and I've been me ever
> since. Just being me, knowing that if I'm me and I lead with
> my heart. I'm not trying to satisfy this person or that person,
> I am just going to be true to myself. I care deeply. But, when
> I'm honest with them and say, hey, do you know how much I
> care about you? Do you know how much I've thought about
> you? Do you know what my life's like? I'm with you more than
> I'm with my wife and kids. When I'm more like that…more
> in my heart, I don't care about wins and losses that much. I
> just love coaching. I love being in a relationship with kids who
> are going for something that is big. I love being a part of that.
> That's the bottom line. (Rick)

Importance of Relationships:
"They Don't Get Part of Me; They Get All of Me"

As Coach Malnati recalled the players throughout his coaching journey, the importance of these relationships drove much of his decision processes. Wins, championships, awards, and professional resume are all important in the life of a coach, but none of these compare to the lifelong relationships Rick valued with his players:

I could never just coach basketball without the relationships that come with it. When my relationships with the kids are off, I don't like it. I just don't like what I'm doing. If we're not seeing eye-to-eye, and it happens a little bit, it's uncomfortable. I can still coach, but there's something off; I'm not on full stride. If I'm doing something where I think a kid thinks we're at odds, it bugs me to death, or if I see that with my kids I'm very confrontational when they don't get along and I make them go after each other probably in a way they've never experienced before. I don't care if you don't like the kid but if you hate him then why do you hate him? What does he need to change? It's important to have heart-to-heart talks and know what kids are going through. You've got kids every year that are struggling with things that are so much bigger than basketball. But, that probably gives me the most satisfaction is when you listen to a kid talk and a kid's crying about something that's going on in his life and it's brutal. But, you're there to say that it's going to be okay. (Rick)

His candor and confrontational demand for honesty tested his players, but tended to build camaraderie that lasts long beyond playing careers:

I've asked right after a season, how was I? Did I just screw you guys up or did you guys have any fun? The year we came in fourth in state, I thought I drove those guys hard. I've hammered them and been on them. I said something to Romie and he said it was great, and I said something to Teddy Rosinski and he said it was awesome and great. The kids know me; they're around me…they know me, and one of the goals is to have relationships with those guys forever, too. Also, that they feel like they can come back…that this is a family kind of atmosphere. Once a New Trier basketball player, always a New Trier basketball player. (Rick)

Rick respected the power that basketball wields in its ability to alter perspectives and literally change lives. Riley (1993) offered the following perspective:

> Teamwork is the essence of life. It makes possible everything from moonshots to the building of cities to the renewal of life. The key to teamwork is to learn a role, accept that role, and strive to become excellent playing it. "Act well your part," Shakespeare wrote, "therein lies the glory."

Rick continued to share a significant story about the life-changing power of relationships in basketball:

> The key is always going to be teamwork. An example would be Todd Townsend transfers into New Trier. Todd is a kid that was ruled ineligible. They went to court and they got a temporary restraining order that said that he could play, but if he's found ineligible, you'll forfeit all of your games. So, what would you expect the normal 18-year-old kid to say that has been in the program when that was proposed to them? Do they say, okay, let's not let Todd play with us, you know, let's wait, or do they say, hey, look at my life...I cannot believe my life and look at what Todd's been through? They might take away our wins but they'll never take away our memories. We're going to support Todd 100% and if we lose, we lose but we're doing it with Todd playing. And, for those kids to say that aloud and come to my office and tell me that, I was like...oh, I can't believe it! You guys get it, you know, this is what it's about, who cares how many games we win, but who can take away the memories that we have together! Then, when Todd was going to court, we would actually meet before school and the kids would actually pray for Todd. Now, you can't do that in school, but we'd be down in the locker room in the basement and the kids would say prayers for Todd. We weren't at court with him, but

we were praying for him. And then, to see Todd now, he's the benefit of having great teammates that year. And, that's going to play out in those kids' lives multiple times. They'll always be connected. Somehow they'll always be connected. That year was a powerful year. There were so many things going on. It's pretty cool, the guys are doing different things now…guys are investment bankers, guys are in medical school…it was a pretty awesome year. (Rick)

Vision: Prepare for State

Rick possessed a powerful skill for conveying his vision. The day after New Trier lost in a regional final, he called me to prepare for my team's next opponent, Loyola Academy. He shouted over the phone, "I know Loyola, better than Loyola knows Loyola. Meet me in my office." When I arrived, he unveiled his preparation for Loyola throughout the season. He had multiple tapes, multiple scouting reports, and sheets that identified their verbal and non-verbal signals. Within ten minutes, I knew we would defeat Loyola. Rick's aura of confidence breathed hope and clarity into my understanding of Loyola. When most coaches lick their wounds after a season-ending defeat, Rick found the time, energy, and friendship to help me prepare my team, the Wildkits, who are the Trevians' nemesis. This friendship repeated itself throughout the years I competed against Rick. I don't know a more generous man.

Rick's countenance beamed when he spoke about the Trevians' Super-sectional victory over #1-seeded Proviso East featuring Dee and Shannon Brown. Rick said, "Part of me thought we had no chance, yet another part of me thought we could do it and these kids have got to know. I told my kids throughout the game we're just tougher." Malnati began preparation for the state tournament in the spring of the year before. He carefully evaluated who his team must beat to win the sectional and built his vision for that team based upon his findings. According to Rick, "The state tournament is where the memories are."

My Favorite Rick Malnati Story

In 2006, Rick joined the fight to build the marrow donor base in an inspired effort to save Coach Steve Pappas's life. Rick led much of that crusade, helping to raise hundreds of thousands of dollars in less than three months. He lent his fund raising expertise honed from his family business, organized the silent auction, recruited WGN's David Kaplan to serve as emcee, and basically created and designed the "Teammates for Life Celebration" honoring Steve Pappas.

I'll never forget his presence at a Team Pappas meeting in March 2006 at Deerfield High School (DHS). Steve's crowded classroom was jam packed with Steve's friends and family, Steve's former players, his DHS colleagues, and an army of coaches dedicated to save Steve's life. After introductions and learning about Steve's prognosis, the need for a marrow drive and its astronomical costs became clear. At fifty dollars per screening and the odds of a match for Steve at one in ten thousand, we needed hope, but more importantly a plan. Discussion included bake sales, t-shirt drives, coaching clinics, raffles, and other offerings; then a gentle, soft-spoken woman who had championed drives for other cancer patients outlined the strategy of donation canisters placed on counters in stores and restaurants. All of the suggestions were valuable, sincere, and hopeful, but I saw the frustration boiling in Rick's tortured visage. He realized how grave Steve's condition was and fully understood the urgent picture. For the first time that night Rick spoke. Actually, Rick shouted. "I respect all of your ideas, but we need a Super Bowl plan! If you could do anything, money being no object, what would you do to save Steve's life right now?" His raw and alarming pitch stunned the room. His harsh tone caused us initially to retreat, but forced us to reach beyond our current capabilities. His presentation defined Rick. He thought big, saw big, and was committed to big. Rick suggested we draft a team of doctors and nurses, equip them with supplies, charter a plane to Steve's native land of Greece where the likelihood of a donor was significantly enhanced, and bribe every person of Greek heritage to submit to a marrow test until we find the match. We were awed by his passion, overwhelmed by his generosity, and inspired by his confidence. His players must think him insane at times with his big demands and impatience with timid thinking. His intolerance for anything but the very best is a quality inherent in many of our world's most influential people from Beethoven to Lombardi. Rick coached us that night. He demanded us to rally together to achieve a lofty goal just as he rallied the student/athletes of New Trier High School.

A New Malnati Chapter

Rick Malnati stunned the Chicago high school basketball community when he announced his resignation from New Trier High School in April 2008. His twelve years of fierce leadership bettered the lives of thousands. In 2011, Rick accepted the assistant basketball coach position at Loyola University Chicago. In 2013 he returned to high school hoops as the coach at Fenwick High School in Oak Park, Illinois.

CHAPTER FIVE

●

GENE PINGATORE:
ST. JOSEPH HIGH SCHOOL

"You've got to be yourself"

G ene Pingatore, arguably the most successful basketball coach in Chicago history, steadily impacted the basketball world and all of its permutations through five decades of good old-fashioned hard work. Listening to Coach Pingatore regale his perspectives on life, coaching, and sense of duty affirmed why this very "real" and plain spoken man met with such remarkable success. Born in 1936, "Ping" experienced life in urban America during much of its character building growth. From the Great Depression to WWII, to the Cold War, to Civil Rights, to the Space Age, to Viet Nam, to Watergate, to the Computer Age, and into the Millenium, he had been loyally accompanied by one of his dearest friends, the wonderful game of basketball. Before becoming the "Dean" of Illinois High School Basketball, Gene: (a) played in "The 1954 City Championship" where St. Mel upset DuSable, igniting race riots at jam-packed Chicago Stadium pressuring the CPS to ban night games; (b) dogged the now President of the Phoenix Suns, Jerry Colangelo during AAU competitions; (c) had his corner jump shot swatted by USF's Bill Russell in a college tournament game; (d) pitched for the legendary Sobie's team of Chicago sixteen inch Clincher Softball; (e) owned Pingatore's, a suburban restaurant favorite; (f) launched the college basketball careers of hundreds, including Isiah Thomas, Amal McCaskill, Jeff Hornacek, Tom Miller, Marty Clark, Tony Freeman, Tony Freeman Junior, Evan Turner, Demetri McCamey, Daryl Cunningham,

Daryl Thomas, and Cliff Scales; (g) was misrepresented in the Academy Award winning film *Hoop Dreams*; (h) served St. Joseph High School in Westchester, Illinois as teacher, coach, dean, fund raiser, and principal; and (i) shaped the thinking of thousands of players, coaches, and fans in Chicago who marveled at his commitment to excellence throughout his 51 year reign.

Early Years: The Importance of Family

Taylor Street, the romantically gritty Italian enclave on Chicago's near west side, engenders a story-like aura that has produced many of the Windy City's richest tales. Annette and Frank Pingatore, Gene's parents crossed paths at a Taylor Street fire in 1932 that lit a spark Gene and his family carry to this day. Frank, "Banjo Eyes," was a wise guy destined for trouble until that fateful evening blocks from Mrs. O'Leary's barn where he met the determined and resourceful Annette who demanded love, a life of hard respectable work, and the promise of a healthy family. He committed his devotion to Annette and their family, worked hard his whole life at the Hot Point factory in Cicero, and produced two exceptional children, one of them destined to make his mark on the game played on the hardwood of Chicago. Gene remembered the impact of the depression:

> I was born in 1936. We were just coming out of the depression…and then the war. I remember taking the wagon and going to the firehouse and getting our allotment of dry goods like beans, rice, or whatever. I remember those days when we didn't have anything. Right at the firehouse, that is where things were rationed. In the neighborhood, that was the clearinghouse for people to pick up food.

> I remember ration stamps. We didn't have a car. Everything we did was on public transportation. And, yet, it was not like we were poor. We were hardworking people like everybody else and you made it. That's the kind of background I come from—workin'. Yet, my grandfather on my mom's side was from the aristocracy in Italy. He was an architect and came to

> this country and became a general contractor and became a
> very wealthy man. When the Depression hit, like everybody
> else, he lost everything. (Gene)

On top of the pain of the wartime economy, young Gene, ever the incendiary, provided a fresh challenge to the Pingatores when he burned down the family home:

> I was a little kid. It was a Saturday. I'll never forget it. Mom
> and Dad were shopping and my great-grandmother was
> taking care of my sister, Sandy, and myself. I had to be seven
> and Sandy was four or five. We were listening to the radio,
> either Tarzan or something because there was no TV, not that
> early. I said to my sister, "Let's go explore the jungle." So I lit a
> candle and we go into my closet. In the closet, my mother had
> hung curtains from the cleaners, wrapped in cellophane that
> she hadn't put up yet. My great-grandmother came yelling and
> screaming. She was in the kitchen frying Italian sausage for
> my grandfather. So what do you think? She fills the frying pan
> with the grease up with water to throw on the fire. The whole
> thing went up in flames. We lost everything. (Gene)

Gene's grandfather, who methodically rebuilt his contractor business, welcomed Gene's family into his home until the Pingatores got back on their feet. This random catastrophe served to strengthen an already close knit extended family, and forged traditions that the Pingatore clan supports to this day. Coach Pingatore recreated these family dynamics through his teams for half of a century. Respect, trust, loyalty, and brotherhood all stemmed from his foundational understanding of his own family:

> The secret for us was that's the way we were brought up. I
> looked at family as more than family. I enjoyed their company.
> They were like friends. We enjoyed doing things together. One
> of the greatest nights of the year for us is Christmas Eve at my

sister's house. We have like 30 people who have been there at Christmas Eve with all the fish. We still live up to the traditions of the past where there was a fast day. We fast all day until dinner, fast in abstinence for meat on Christmas Eve. That's not the case in the church anymore, but we still do that. The tradition comes from my parents and my aunts and the kids now have picked it up. Prior to that, it was my grandparents doing it and that's how you build all that stuff. We still do it. When I'm gone, I'm sure the kids are going to do it. (Gene)

I naively asked coach what the fish of choice is at the Pingatores' Christmas Eve gala. He responded with a smile and answered in great detail:

It's not just *the* fish! On that day, my sister's sons, her daughter-in-laws, and my daughter go over and help prepare all the food and then we come back and we eat at 7:00 o'clock at night. We have appetizers and baked clams, calamari, and salmon. Then we go with linguini with black mussels, baccala, and squid. She puts lobster in there and besides that all, the pasta with all that stuff in there. Then we have fried baccala; we have Alaskan king crab. We have smelt. Then we have all kinds of shrimp and all kinds of salads. We eat until it's time for everyone to go their separate ways to midnight mass, or whatever, and then they come back. Then the next day we go to somebody else's house to have dinner. (Gene)

I included these depictions of Pingatore family life because of their relevance to the approach Gene shared with his student/athletes. His face lit up as he described his family traditions, crowded dinner tables, noisy kitchens, and animated discussions. He treated his teams as families and tried to replicate the energy of his Italian roots and what went into preparation for special occasions. The St. Joseph Chargers enjoyed hundreds of special occasions in the form of championship games.

Coach Pingatore's humble beginnings and his perceptions of his folks' struggles helped to shape his relationship with basketball. He undoubtedly agreed with the following words from former Chicago Bulls coach, Phil Jackson:

> Life, like basketball, is messy and unpredictable. It has its way
> with you, no matter how hard you try to control it. The trick is
> to experience each moment with a clear mind and open heart.
> When you do that, the game—and life—will take care of itself.

While most high school basketball coaches are preoccupied with Holiday Tournament preparation, Ping hung tight to his family and understood that his career, built on those same family principles, has its place…just not on December 24th. He credited his mother for shaping his principled approach to life:

> Mom. Unbelievable. If she was a man, she would have been the
> president of the United States. She was a dynamo. Hard worker.
> I think I got most of it from her. My dad was a hard worker,
> but never said much. He wasn't motivated to be better; He was
> satisfied. My mom was never satisfied. And I'm not. You might
> think that with being the way I am, I should have moved on to
> college basketball coaching. But that wasn't important. Timing
> was the reason why I didn't. I had a desire to do all that stuff,
> but the timing wasn't right because of family. I didn't want to
> leave them and leave my mom and my daughter. But I did learn
> that whatever I do, I want to do the best I can. That's the only
> way and I've tried to teach that to the people around me. (Gene)

In Frosty Westerings' book, *Make the Big Time Where You Are,* this concept of being the best you can be regardless of the role affirms Ping's philosophy and supports his unyielding dedication to his students. He was firmly grounded. College and pro coaches constantly adorn the front page stories detailing scandal, deceit, greed, and moral confusion. Gene was loyal to his family, himself, and his mission. This uncomplicated simplicity navigated him safely through the choppy waters of ego, competition, and temptation.

I asked coach to share a story that would paint a picture of his remarkable mother and he provided this portrait:

> She was a stickler on keeping the house clean, picked up. My sister and I were doing things in the house as young kids that people in their 20s today won't even do. I was painting walls as a grade school kid. I was fixing things. I was learning how to cook. Both my sister and I did all that stuff. Do you know what? It's a shame that more people don't teach that to their kids today. She taught us about working hard and taught us about keeping things nice.

> One day, a neighbor brought her two kids over. Well, her kids were terrors and my age. The two kids were standing on the couch trying to swing from the drapes. My mom walked in. She hollered at them, but who do you think she really got on? Me! Because how could I allow that? She literally picked up the rocker and broke the sucker over my back. She was tough. She was the disciplinarian. My dad was always working. He had the second shift. He was always working from 3 to 11. So I rarely saw him. I was at school and when I came home it was my mom. Very demanding and I think that's where I pick up all my traits for the most part. (Gene)

Hard working, stickler for details, intelligent, unsatisfied, demanding, disciplined, and dynamic were traits chosen by Gene to describe his mother. I'll bet his players and colleagues would describe Gene the same way. In his celebrated book, *Lincoln on Leadership*, Donald Phillips recognized that a highly disproportionate number of the world's greatest leaders came from homes of absent fathers and remarkably strong mothers.

After speaking about the importance of family in his life and emphasizing how loyal his Mom was to the preservation of that family, he recalled a disconcerting visit back to California he made a year after his graduation from Loyola University of California:

> It's different out there. People aren't close and I was used to family and friends. I went back and visited. We got everybody together and I found out that was the first time that the California people had gotten together since I left. That bothered me. They didn't see each other. I was used to all the stuff we've been talking about [family and friends] and I didn't like that. The place [California] was great and all that, but I would have been a lonely man. So I came back to Chicago and never did go back. (Gene)

The Pride of Cicero: Exposure to Basketball

Coach Pingatore credited much of his success as a coach to his days as a boy on the streets, play lots, and gyms of Cicero, Illinois. He began playing basketball in seventh grade and met with the devastation of being cut from the team:

> I think a lot of my motivation as a coach comes from what I did as a youngster as far as playing. I was always blessed in being for the most part on good teams and I was used to winning. Winning becomes a habit and as a result, if you've always been on good teams and are used to winning, you're going to carry that over when you coach. I was always like that. I started playing basketball as a 7th grader. I went out for my… in those days it was just one team—8th grade team at Cicero School and I got cut. They had one pair of pants left and it was between me and another kid; I was devastated. (Gene)

The setback inspired him to practice, play, and educate himself into a ball player. Gene reflected: "The biggest thing I remember was shootin'. I used to go find kids to play against in the schoolyard and that's it. We'd play until dark and go home. I was content. I never even gave it a thought."

Young Gene earned a place on the eighth grade team the next year and continued his quest to get better. Cicero was rife with role models but what really grabbed Gene's attention was the raw athleticism and competitive league play at the Western Electric Basketball League, featuring former all state and college athletes who played in-house on their huge factory compound. Gene said, "Those were the people I watched. I really fell in love with the game. I'd sit there every Friday night and just watch all the games and I'd dream about playing basketball."

St. Mel? Unlikely Encounter with Gentleman Jim Weaver

Gene was a public school kid from Cicero School and assumed he'd matriculate to Morton High School, which happened to be the number one ranked basketball program in the state in 1951; instead, Gene found his way to St. Mel High School on the Westside of Chicago, a school and network of people that one day would connect him to playing in the city championship game at Chicago Stadium, to college at Loyola University of California, to a career in education, to St. Joseph High School, to Isiah Thomas, and to the thousands of people who helped build the Pingatore legacy.

> How did I get to St. Mel? I didn't know anything about St. Mel. One of the guys I hung around with in grade school, who wasn't an athlete but just a guy I hung around with—Jimmy Cichon—talked my parents into sending me to St. Mel because he was going. I don't know why I even agreed with it. They said this is where you're going to go. I took the test. I ended up going to St. Mel. I didn't know anybody there except Jimmy Cichon. Two months into the school year, he got kicked out of school and there I was. I went out for basketball and made the Bantam [JV] team. My eventual varsity coach, Jim Weaver, coached me. He had just come over from St. Pat's. He had won the city with Pat Dunn at Pat's the year before.

By my junior year, I played forward on the varsity. I was 5'11½" to 6 feet. I made All-South Section. In my senior year, the coach came up to me and said: "I'm not going to start you. Okay. We have to start Mike Caracelli, who was 6'7" for us to be good." I'll never forget the conversation. He said: "Even though he's starting and you're not, I still consider you a starter." As it turned out, I probably played more than he did or other guys because I was the first guy off the bench. So I came off the bench as a senior and he must have known what he was doing because we won the city championship that year.

Because Catholic schools weren't allowed to participate in the state tournament, the city championship was what we played for. The legendary DuSable team was our opponent. Some say the best team that ever came out of Chicago. We kicked their butts. Paxton Lumpkin, Sweet Charlie Brown, Charlie McMillan. Chicago Stadium! Standing room only! Unbelievable!

You want to talk about me being a nutcase? A Friday night game at Chicago Stadium and we're playing for the state championship. Okay? The game was an 8:00 o'clock game because they had the 3rd place game before. What do you think I was doing at 6:00 o'clock on that Friday night? I'm playing in Cicero in an all-star game. It was a big thing in those days. We used to pack the Cicero stadium. I got done playing and we won that game. My mother had a cab waiting to get me to the Chicago Stadium. But get this? I can't get in. It was so jammed. I can't get in. Some priest saw me trying to get in and recognized me. He said come with me and that's how we got in. I was late to the locker room and got dressed.

> Think about me as the coach finding out one of my kids…I would go goofy. (Gene)

Coach Pingatore's animated eyes brightened when he reflected upon his high school experience and his ambitious coach, Jim Weaver, who kept Gene and his teammates hopping both in and out of season:

> Jim Weaver always had us scrimmage during the summer against his former players from Pat's who were now college players and used to kick our butts. It all paid off.

> We used to call him "Gentleman Jim." He never hollered. I learned from his example to be your own personality; otherwise, they see through that. If you're a screamer, be a screamer. But if you're not, don't be a screamer because they'll know it's phony. That's about being a teacher. (Gene)

Go West Young Man: College Years

After a stellar high school basketball career, Gene weighed his college options and leaned toward studying medicine at Loyola University of Los Angeles:

> The whole thing was Jim Weaver thought he was going to get the head coaching position at Loyola of Los Angeles. He was a coach on the move but didn't get it. Yet I ended up going to Loyola Los Angeles despite Coach Weaver's fate. The following year, he got the job at Saint Mary's in Moraga, California. I had to play against him. He got two of my teammates up there with him and I ended up playing against two of my teammates, Andy Sloan and Mike Caroselli. He left there and became the first coach of the Houston Chaparelles of the ABA.

> I was a forward in high school. I went to college and now I'm playing guard. I never developed into a great ball handler, but I was smart. And if you're not a great ball handler then

don't handle it. Am I right? I try to tell kids, you gotta do what you gotta do. What I did do was I became an excellent defender. (Gene)

Gene competed against one of the most celebrated defenders in basketball history and recalled his memory with humor:

When I was a sophomore, Bill Russell and San Francisco won the conference title again and we took second again. But I got in the game. We were getting killed. It was one of those: He's not going to block this shot. I was on this side in the corner and he was way over. I said: You're not going to block this shot. The friggin' ball ended up in the second floor balcony. (Gene)

Gene went on to recall the events that precipitated his decision to reconsider his career path and choice of study:

I should have graduated in '58, but I changed my major in my junior year. I was in pre-med for three years. I was doing okay until my junior year and not all schools have that. They have what they call elimination courses for pre-med to knock people out that go to medical school. That happened to be Quantitative Analysis at Loyola. The difference in making it was that you had to spend many, many more hours in the lab outside the class to do it. I passed it, but saw that this was only one hurdle in a long race. So now I'm at a decision of what did I want? Do I want basketball or do I want to be a doctor? Obviously, I chose basketball which was a good thing. To be a doctor, you've got to want it. You've really got to want it. You can't do that half ass. I didn't want it bad enough. When I made that change is when I decided I wanted to coach. (Gene)

The St. Joseph Connection: A Star is Born

That fateful career course correction began another chapter in the life of the hopeful, soon to be Coach Pingatore:

> When I got back home from college it was March of 1959. There was a big sign on this property, right here [St. Joseph High School]. Christian Brothers. That was me. Building a high school. I said: Great! So I went to St. Mel, found some of the Christian Brothers that were still there that knew me, asked for their support, and applied for the job at St. Joe's. I had no education courses, so in September '59 through '60, I went back to school here [Chicago] at Loyola and DePaul. I ended up getting all my education courses out of the way that year. Now, a big stumbling block occurs at the end of that year. I got drafted.
>
> By that time, I had already signed my contract to teach at St. Joe's. I contacted my local congressman, Collier. I'll never forget. I said: "Is there anything that can be done about this? I've already signed up to teach at St. Joe's and I just got drafted." He said: "Let me check it out." Guess what? The key was that I had the contract signed before I got drafted. So as it turned out I got the job. They opened their doors here in the fall of 1960 and I've been here ever since. (Gene)

After nine years of teaching history and assisting Coach Pat Callahan, Gene Pingatore assumed the role of Head Coach midseason of 1969. Callahan had a falling out with administration and resigned. Gene explained: "And he actually did it to give me a chance because he felt that, if he finished the season, then administration would open up the job and I wouldn't have a chance to get the job."

It's hard to imagine St. Joseph High School without Gene Pingatore, let alone that he may have been passed over for a "better" coach. Was Red Auerbach leaving Boston? Gene wasted no time in charting his course to resuscitate the moribund Chargers:

> When I took over we were coming off three seasons of…3-20.
> Often times with coaches, and I'm sure I fell into that pattern,
> they think they're going to be successful just because of their
> innate coaching ability. It takes more than that. It takes talent,
> too. And I knew that. I knew that just from my experience of
> playing that you've got to have players. So the very first thing
> that I did was go out and recruit. (Gene)

The word "recruiting" bears an unsavory connotation in high school sports. For years, Catholic schools have assertively marketed their product to neighboring parochial school students and any other families willing to embrace Catholic school philosophy and pay tuition. Once St. Joseph established itself as a powerhouse, sending many of its graduates to Division I schools on scholarships, basketball players from all over Chicagoland travelled to the sleepy town of Westchester, IL. Like other successful coaches, Gene Pingatore had been accused of unethical recruiting. Dominant success tends to breed jealous scrutiny. Fortunately for St. Joe's, success also breeds more success and as the Chargers blossomed, school enrollment increased commensurately. Recruiting and marketing are the life blood of Catholic schools.

By 1975, the Chargers were for real. NBC television's game of the week featured a showdown with ESCC rival St. Patrick. The immediate importance of victory was overshadowed by a more enduring phenomenon of the recruiting variety:

> We packed this place. We're blowing Pat's out in the first half
> and ended up holding on to win knocking St. Pat's out of the
> conference title hunt. But the key to that whole game was the
> fact that a little guy by the name of Isiah Thomas was in the
> audience and that game inspired him into coming to St. Joe's.
> He loved the spirit and all the hype and the whole thing.

I didn't know him. I hadn't recruited that area. His class was the first time I ever attempted to recruit Resurrection grade school. I didn't even know about Isiah. I was going after Tyrone Brewer. Everybody knew about Tyrone. When I went to see Tyrone play, Isiah wasn't there, so I still didn't know about him. But I did invite them to come to our tournament. That's when I first saw Isiah. All I said as Isiah was coming up the stairs from the locker room was: "Great game." I didn't use his name at the time. I said: "I'd love to have you come to St. Joe's." He looked at me and said: "Okay." (Gene)

Coach laughed while recalling the pure simplicity of that monumental exchange in the stairwell:

So that was my first contact with him and then he must have come to check us out, liked what he saw, and that was it. Of course, there were a number of other circumstances that helped. My principal at the time was Br. Alfred Marshall and he happened to be the principal at St. Mel when a couple of the other Thomas kids went to St. Mel. So they knew him and he knew the family. So all that helped. You know, timing is wonderful in stuff like that. It's a good story. (Gene)

1976 was Isiah's freshman year. Pingatore was tempted to play Isiah on the varsity, but for many reasons kept the talented underclassmen together while he coached both the varsity and the sophomores that season:

So as a result, the '76 seniors played and we were just god awful. I think we won 6 or 7 games. Great kids, but not great players. The sophomore team was dynamite and I coached them both. You talk about a zoo? I coached the sophomore team while the varsity got dressed, and then I had to go down and talk pregame to the varsity while the sophs got dressed. It was unbelievably tough. In practice, I would go from one to the other. In those days, I didn't have a multitude of assistants like I do now. I had the sophomores and varsity. That following year is when I brought in Dennis Doyle as sophomore coach and thankfully he was with me a long time, but that particular year was unbelievably tough. But I did it and I loved it.

If I had moved Isiah up…and I admit if I had a sophomore coach, I might have done that. The '76 team would have been a pretty good team. In '77, we were a lot better with Isiah as a sophomore, but inconsistent. We didn't have the discipline that we eventually had. Shoot, I remember a game we had Marist down by 23 at the half and lost the game at Marist. I'll never forget that. It was Isiah out of control. Ray Clark out of control. They came back the following year and it was totally different. It was amazing. (Gene)

Philosophy: Be Yourself

"I never got up to go to work and said:
'Hey I don't want to go in.' Not one day in 48 years."

Anyone who spent time with Gene Pingatore knew that he was "real." He preached being real, coaches being real, and lived every moment of every day being real. His advice to teachers and coaches was, "<u>Be yourself. The kids will spot a phony a mile away</u>":

How many times have you seen someone trying to be Bobby Knight? You can't do that. You've got to be your own personality. You can't be something you're not. You're going to fail. As a teacher, kids will see through it. As a coach, the players will see through it. Assistants will see through it. You've got to be yourself. And maybe that is not going to be like Bobby Knight and that's okay. You'll still get things done.

> He's the best. I don't care about what everyone else thinks. He's a genius, but there are things that I don't agree with. What I did was I took all the things I agreed with and then I was myself in other things. (Gene)

Ping's formula worked for tens of thousands of Chargers who studied this "old school" yet timeless champion. His raspy voice and no nonsense bespectacled face camouflaged his genuine intention to learn about people, perhaps Gene's most enjoyable diversion.

Gene Pingatore is to Chicagoland basketball as Huck Finn was to the Mississippi. His fearless quest for competitive adventure and pragmatic persona exuded ambition and curiosity. Ping found the game. He surrounded himself with great people and supported whatever environment he built with loyalty, humor, and camaraderie. Whether it was the old neighborhood pick-up teams, Sobie's softball teams, his Friday night card group, his favorite golf foursome, or the champion Chargers, people of all ages valued his company. He was always on the move.

Leadership: Hero Making

> You've got to let your people reign, but yet be able to control. You can't micromanage. You've got to be hands-on a little bit, I think. You've got to show everybody you care, take an interest in them, care about what you're doing, care about this place, care about your job, and care about them. I have to keep my hands involved. People accuse me a lot of wanting to do it myself all the time, that I've got to learn to let other people do it. It was hard in the beginning, but I'm doing that more and more now, as I get older. (Gene)

Coach worked hard to include input from others, but admitted in certain areas, like identifying talent, his instincts trumped the perceptions of his staff:

I'm really good at evaluating talent. Now what does that mean? Everything is in the eye of the beholder. But I just really feel like I can recognize talent more so than my staff and I know that by experience of how they'll promote a kid that they've got to play yet he can't play. Oh, we used to have great arguments. But I really believe that there is something that I can tell about a kid and for the most part I am on target. There were very rare situations that I was not right.

I can tell most of the time when a kid comes walking in, forget about seeing him on a court, just walking down the hall, I can tell if this kid is an athlete by the way he walks and the way he handles himself. It's just the feel I have. So I watch stuff like that and footwork, and selfishness or lack of it. I really want to tell you, I go by feel. I'm also good at reading people. I'm pretty perceptive in recognizing people that are real or not real. (Gene)

Gene's special sense of perception led to unparalleled success. He saw talent in children where others did not. He also anticipated situational conflict and on many occasion clarified potential trouble before people involved recognized that there was trouble. During the time I interviewed Coach Pingatore, I found myself observing details with more scrutiny. On the night of one of our conversations, snow had fallen on the streets of Westchester. When I arrived to take Coach to dinner, he was putting on his overshoes to protect his dress shoes. I noticed that his shoes were older, yet impeccably kept and that his galoshes were of a bygone era. His spectacles were especially shiny, his shirts and sport coats were always freshly pressed, and his hair was never out of place. As my colleague and friend Coach Mike Kolze would say, "Gene knows his horseflesh." Pingatore understood value, maintained value, protected value, and created valuable opportunities. For half a century he parlayed his incredible judgment skills for value into the glory that St. Joseph High School enjoyed. He tended to all matters with an exceptional degree of integrity. When I arrived home after the dinner and interview, I removed my snow soaked and salt stained shoes and was reminded of the wisdom and discipline of Ping.

Success Starts at the Point

Coach Pingatore held special value and appreciation for the important position of point guard on a team:

> I've argued this with friends for years. If I were going to start a professional team and have the choice of all the players in the country, I'd choose a point guard with character. If you have a dynamite point guard and no big guys, you're going to be competitive. If you have dynamite big guys and no guards, you're in trouble.
>
> What is point guard mentality? Unselfish leadership, and on the other hand an ability to take over a game and make the shots when they're needed. You look, you watch, and observe. If it's there (point guard ability) you can refine it and that's the fun of it. And if it's not there, you get through it. You play, but you're not as good as you would have hoped because you lack a strong point guard. (Gene)

At the time of this conversation, the Chicago Bulls had selected Derrick Rose, a point guard with Chicago roots, as the number one pick of the draft. According to Coach Ping's theory, the Bulls should improve. Have they ever!

St. Joe's basketball relied upon the creativity, chutzpah, and intuition of countless point guards over the years. Their strengths allowed Gene to make changes on the fly:

> You watch my teams. The kind of adjustments we make are based on those kinds of things—a feel for the game. I love to go up and press everybody full court the whole game. Now, you'll see a lot of my teams haven't been able to do that

recently. Well, why do you think? Because they couldn't press. They didn't have a feel. Good guards who you would think would be able to pick it up and do those things didn't have it. So what do you do? You don't press. You back off and you still play as best as you can. That's the key. You don't teach that; you refine it. You either have it or you don't. (Gene)

Over the years, I have witnessed creativity and flexibility in the system of play engineered by Gene. When many coaches attempt to shoehorn players into "the system," Ping excelled because of his willingness to tweak his systems to accommodate and accentuate the shortcomings and talents of his charges. Former Bulls' coach Phil Jackson possessed a similar knack: "Find a structure that would empower everybody, not just the stars. And allow the players to grow as individuals as they surrender themselves to the group effort."

Strength in the System: KISS Method

I asked Coach Pingatore to elaborate more on the development and elements of his system for success:

I don't have any secrets. I'm going to run motion. It's a frustration for me this year because some of the players are not sharp. Sometimes you have to stand back and evaluate. I talked to Coach Knight about it because he's been through the same thing. God forbid, we were talking about…playing some zone? He said: "You know what? He's doing it." I said: "Maybe it's not all that bad." I may have to do that because we have guys that aren't capable [of man to man concepts]. Some guys just don't pick it up. It has nothing to do with intelligence. They just don't get it. Yet sometimes I step back and say: "The track record of success for doing what we've been doing has been pretty good, so let's not tweak it too much. Let's stay with what we're doing and if we want to add a little bit in a certain situation." So I do that to myself. I talk to myself, but I also talk to the assistants to see what they think. Sometimes I talk to Knight or someone like that just to get an opinion.

As a young coach, I taught what I knew, but everything became a gimmick. Gimmick this, gimmick that. Change with the wind or I'd pick up something new. There was no consistency. I think the turning point for our program, besides Isiah, was when we decided to follow Bobby Knight's stuff. I went to his camps and learned that the best thing was to keep it simple—the KISS [Keep It Simple Stupid] method. Once we did that and stayed true to it we started getting good because then we were able to teach it better; the kids knew it better. We weren't always changing and gimmicking it. If you're teaching a multitude of different things, how well will the kids do any one of them as opposed to teaching something that [you teach] over and over and you get them to do it really well? That happened in 1978. That was our first year that we really got in motion and stuck with the press. We don't vary much. We don't have a lot of special plays. Shoot, it's not like playing Denny Zelasko [former coach of Notre Dame High School] with his X's and O's. God almighty! In our conference, we felt we were so prepared to play people non-con and in the tournament because it was such a tough, tough thing to compete in the East Suburban Catholic conference. Unbelievable.

For us, we keep it simple. We finally arrived at a philosophy in what we were going to do and we just stayed with it. (Gene)

Gene's life experience allowed him to genuinely and confidently accept the KISS method. Paying his dues over the decades afforded him a special understanding of what works and what doesn't. Like many teachers, he constantly searched for better resources, approaches, and strategies, but his long career provided him time to truly examine a wealth of systems and arrive at one that made sense to him. Very few coaches survive long enough in their careers to attain the confidence that Coach Pingatore employed.

Throughout our conversations, Coach emphasized the value of repetition, refinement, and attentiveness to detail. Most coaches espouse these tenets, but Ping recognized the critical kinship between systematic play and details:

> From the beginning, I've always had a very competitive nature. Not that I am all the time, but I always wanted to be the best I could be and do the best I could do. I've been accused of being a...What do they call it, OCD [obsessive-compulsive disorder]? I believe in little things and when they are not done, it bothers me. I like my practice broken down by minutes because I've got to get things done, but I often get carried away and spend more time on something than I should. If I can't do the best I can, I don't want to do it at all. I've always been that way. (Gene)

From his teen days of recruiting park teams on the play lots of Cicero and later softball players for Sobies, Gene learned perhaps the most important detail when building teams, and directed his Charger teams accordingly:

> Do you know what the key to our success was? It was the fact that we didn't have a bunch of jackasses to play with us. They had to fit because, when it was all said and done, it was the relationships that you developed with those people. We were good because we were talented, but we were good because we really bonded. To this day, those are my best friends. (Gene)

The Priority of Self-Discipline: No "I" in Team

John Wooden reminded coaches of perhaps their most important responsibility: "The powerful influence of example should be a sacred trust for all of those who are in the position to help mold the character of young people." Coach Pingatore guided many novice coaches through the framework of prioritization:

I had a grade school coach come to me recently. We do that little Kansas drill before we go into the locker room. From up in the stands it looks great. It looks like people running all over, passing and cutting. "Coach, how do you get your kids to do that? I wish you could show me." I said: "I want to tell you what. The first thing you've got to do is you've got to make them [your players] pick up the candy wrappers." There are candy wrappers all over the locker room and his team was down there. They'd just thrown them on the floor. But I meant it. How can you get them to do the Kansas Drill if you can't get them to do a simple thing?

So, I'm still a stickler and it works a lot with most players and I don't give in. I'm a stickler about our kids all taking showers. It doesn't happen today elsewhere [at other schools], but my friggin' kids take a shower. They have to wear a jock. We do periodic jock checks. Coach; check the jocks or 25 stairs. You've got to be clean-shaven. Does that make the kid a bad kid? No, but I tell them: "This is the way it is. You're going to wear a jock. Starting tomorrow the first day, make sure you have a jock. We're going to check. Be clean-shaven. Okay? Haircut." The school rules always helped with all that stuff, too. How they dress? When we leave the locker room, every corridor is picked up. I don't go for that bullshit of when you take your tape off and throw it on the floor. "Coach, I didn't do it." We're picking it up together and if we don't do that, 25 stairs. The whole team does stairs. <u>The whole team together</u>. I'm trying to get the other kids to help them police the whole thing. I really think the discipline thing is important. Sometimes they think I've beaten them and that I go too far. But, how do you compromise? If you don't set those kinds of rules, kids will do whatever they want to do. I can't have that. The whole thing breaks down. They have to wear a tie to the games. I'm sure a lot of coaches do all that stuff. We're trying to instill the discipline that it takes to become a good team player. (Gene)

Life Balance: Teaching Spills into Your Life

Countless coaches have tried to reduce the work necessary to build champions. In Chicago, the level of coaching acumen is so extremely competitive that less committed coaches soon learn they can't keep pace. If you choose to coach, you must choose the all-consuming and unreasonable commitment to time and energy:

> People outside of coaching don't understand the commitment that you're making to those kids and to what you're doing. It's so much more than X's and O's. I get questioned about that all the time. I just can't do it any other way. This is my job and I've got to do it this way. I'd have a guilt trip. (Gene)

The more I learn of the life of Gene Pingatore, the more I am affirmed that there are no short cuts. The aura surrounding St. Joseph basketball didn't just happen by accident. The man never stopped working.

Gene couldn't remember the last time he asked his staff to cover for his absence: "The only time that ever happened was if I was sick and I never got sick. I only get sick after the season. I do. The season's over and bam, I get the flu."

When he was able to turn off the basketball switch, Gene enjoyed his solitude, but not for long. Next to spending time with his grand kids, he cherished a number of pastimes:

> I like gardening. I lose myself in my rose and vegetable garden. I've got tons of roses. I love working and then seeing results, so I enjoy it. Tomatoes [Gene was renowned for his home-made tomato sauce cooked ultra-slow over low heat for hours], broccoli, and beans; I freeze all that stuff. It's great therapy, too. I can lose myself with that. I'm not a great golfer, but I

> like to golf. I like to fish. I like the movies. I like all that stuff. I
> like to go out to dinner. I like watching sports on television. I
> watch the NBA, college basketball, and college football. In the
> off season, we'll gamble once a month. And I go to Vegas once
> a year. Even though I enjoy the stuff I do at home, I'm not a
> stay-at-home guy. I like doing stuff. (Gene)

As Gene Pingatore, the winningest coach in Illinois history, described
activities that brought balance to his life, I expected lavish expenditures, exotic
trips, and high profile experiences commensurate with a man that has achieved
so much. Instead, I got a basic KISS lesson in happiness. He would never be
distracted by superfluity. He maintained life-long friendships with regular
people, relished the simplistic artistry of a five hour tomato sauce, and perhaps,
most importantly, enjoyed his own company. His own sense of happiness allowed
him to be accessible to those who needed him, an important quality for a teacher.

Commitment: No Short Cuts

If Malnati was wired for energy and adrenaline and Pappas was wired for
humanity, Pingatore was definitely wired for his allegiance to responsibility.
Coaching requires exceptional commitment:

> Every job that I ever had, be it coaching basketball or running
> a program at school, I've always told my staff: "I can't do it half
> ass. I've got to go all the way with it or I'm not going to do it at
> all." And that's the way I feel about coaching, although I love
> it because I love the game. But as far as working at it, that's
> just the way I am. That's my classroom. It's got to be all the
> way. You've got to make a commitment. That's my philosophy.
> Do the best job you can and you've got to like what you do if
> you're going to do the best job you can. (Gene)

"Students Give You What You Expect"

The one steady constant in the half century of basketball dominance at St. Joseph High School was the ever-optimistic Tony Bennett look-alike, crooning his directions from the sidelines.

Coach Pingatore never sat. At the time of this study, he was seventy-one-years-young and he entered the gym with his team twenty minutes prior to tip off, paced the floor near the scorers' table exchanging lineups and pleasantries with the clock and book officials—both home and away—who admired Gene for decades, barked out his pre-game strategy via his raspy staccato syllables and rhythmic gesticulations, and began his pensive meandering up and down the sideline until the horn sounds.

All time out and dead ball huddles took place twenty feet onto the floor where Ping instructed, reminded, and scolded his standing players who circled him with proud posture and engaged eye-contact.

Coach Steve Pappas carefully studied huddles. He learned a lot about team unity and individual players' characters by watching a team's huddle. St. Joe's huddle on a Saturday matinee game at Loyola University would have impressed Steve. The entire coaching staff and student managers clad in sports coats, pressed shirts, and ties, players consistently uniformed, and the overall energy of these huddles—businesslike and cooperative—exuded a healthy learning environment. Modern culture celebrates individuality and egotistical hubris. The consistent maturity demonstrated during these brief team meetings was not happenstance, but rather a reflection of the level of detail and expectation demanded from the moment hopeful Chargers entered the doors as freshman candidates. In many cases, these scholar athletes learned the St. Joe's culture during grade school experiences as fans, campers, visitors, and siblings of older players. I learned the culture and pedagogy through my constant visits to Westchester.

How I Met Gene Pingatore

As a young freshman coach in 1983, I worked under the direction of legendary Max Kurland of St. Patrick High School. Max would amble with that Kurland gait up to my English classroom and assign my scout duties for the week ahead. I was fascinated by the St. Joe's program: up tempo, physical, man to man denial, complemented by disciplined, yet creative guard play executed by Isiah Thomas clones with explosive quickness and stellar handling skills. Max quickly realized that wherever Joe's played was where I wanted to scout. Early on, I would try to convince Max that the Chargers were our main threat and my repetitive visits would secure us the depth of knowledge to unseat them as perennial champs. Coach Kurland saw right through my ruse, yet in his wisdom, supported my desire to see the best show in town. He knew I would deliver an accurate report on Joe's as well as provide a comparative analysis articulating the various strategies employed by the rest of the conference.

Back in the eighties, St. Joseph had an awful pep band, but they were always spirited, loud, and fanatic about their team. They helped to create an unpleasant ambience for opposing teams and fans. Tile floor, tight rims, dim lighting, and the drone of the hapless band were irritants that accentuated the discomfort meted out by the slicing quickness and the relentless heat from the proud and machine-like Chargers. Midway through the third quarter, the red, black, and white jerseyed warriors hummed and bounced their way to victory. Opponents were typically flushed of color, breathless, and overwhelmingly defeated. Watching Ringmaster Gene's teams play inspired me to develop the system my teams would eventually employ. I knew what good basketball looked like.

When I became a head coach, many of the lessons learned while studying Coach Pingatore's teams I shared with my students at St. Ignatius and Evanston: loyalty to the system, frugal possessions balanced with defense initiated fast breaks, smothering defensive pressure turning dribblers in multiple directions and denying access to entry pass locations, and wing entry denial coupled with rotating help defense from the weak side, leading to off balance shots from opponents resulting in strong block outs and effective defensive rebounds.

St. Joe's played the game the way it should be played. When we [St. Ignatius] earned our first sectional appearance, I was thrilled and honored to meet with Coach Pingatore and the two other regional champion coaches to discuss sectional week at York High School in Elmhurst, IL. I'll never forget how humble and grateful Coach Pingatore was that morning. This was my first taste of the sectional experience. I was jacked, but Ping was every bit as excited, even though this was the latest of almost twenty Regional championships for him and the Chargers. He asked me as we left that meeting with that magical grin of his, "Isn't this fun?" My relationship with the great Coach Pingatore changed that moment. I would always respect and admire his legendary work, but that morning I learned of his *likeability* when conveying his thoughts. I like Gene Pingatore and am fortunate to have crossed paths with this inspiring man.

Defense! Create Discomfort

Any description of the St. Joseph Chargers basketball program must begin with defense. From his days as a college and AAU competitor, Gene Pingatore understood the value of discomfort. "Turn him! Turn him! Make him go left! Make him go left!" were exhortations bellowing from the St. Joe's coaching staff on any given game night. As a player, Pingatore tortured opponents' weaknesses. As a coach, he taught his troops to identify tendencies in foes that revealed inabilities or discomfort zones. If an opposing player could not dribble proficiently with his left hand, the Chargers forced him left. If a team could be pressured to play too fast, here came the Charger heat! Pingatore explained his approach:

> I'm huge on defense. Defensive footwork is just so important. So many kids don't have good footwork. Some of them may not ever get it. It takes three to four years to learn our motion and play our defense. I really believe that. To pick up the habits of really doing it, there is no instant success.

> Kids' talent and repetition, repetition, repetition. It happened with me as a player. I'll never forget playing defense as a

junior for St. Mel. I didn't get it; off the ball defense. I just didn't…it didn't click. Overnight. It was almost like I'm lying in bed and, oh, my God; I understand! That's the way it happens.

I haven't done much 2-2-1 since the 3-point shot came in. The reason is because teams spot up on the arc and beat you at the 3. When we get out of the 2-2-1, we've got to pick up man-to-man. So I've gone more to run and jump and man pressure.

So trying to teach the kids to understand that the rules we do in the half court, we just extend it and now we're just doing something a little more aggressive up front with the same basic rules. So that's it. There's no easy way to do it and teach it. You've just got to get after it and break it down and break it down and that's what we do. (Gene)

One aspect of creating discomfort is the employment of multiple defensive schemes with varying fronts:

It's all a number system. This goes back to when we would zone press. We started it in the Isiah days: #1 was our 2-2-1 zone press and man-to-man; #2 was half-court trap; #3 was just straight man-to-man, pick up at half court. Then when we got into run and jump, #4 was run and jump; #4X was denial inbounds pass, your own man. Then if we did steal it, we stayed in the run and jump. That's why the rotation is so key. You've got to bust your ass. A lot of teams will break the press and try to make that pass under the basket and we're rotating down to steal, right there. I love doing it. It's just frustrating for me when they don't do it as well. (Gene)

Offense: Less is More

Always refining, tweaking, and re-teaching, Pingatore addressed his motion offense with the same meticulous manner that drove the Charger defense. He counted on his lower level coaches to provide repetition, structure, and vernacular to help players graduate seamlessly through the program. Gene, the consummate teacher, mapped it all out:

> It's so simple, it's complex. You teach them the rules. There aren't that many rules. You have rules when you have the ball and you have rules when you don't have the ball. So we give the kids all this stuff, but now to get them to do it is just totally over and over repetition. Stop the play and understand what you've got to do. You've got to teach them to screen. You've got to teach them the V cut and set the man up. It takes time. Over the years, some of them are better than others. It's always that way.

> If their lower level coaches have done it exactly the way they should have, it's going to be a lot easier for me. When they don't, it becomes a problem. For example, I've had coaches over the years at the lower levels that are more concerned about winning the game as opposed to teaching the program stuff. And that's okay in a sense, but what they'll do is put in sets or whatever and that doesn't help me or they'll play kids that I never will play. I've got to be on my toes to watch that kind of stuff. Dennis Doyle was absolutely the best. The kids moved up with him. They were ready to go and it was that easy. (Gene)

The Value of One Possession

Opposing coaches knew to avoid a deficit in the closing minutes of a game against St. Joseph. The Chargers rehearsed these game situations more thoroughly than most; consequently they approached these possession situations with confidence, poise, and an understanding of probability that freed them to play with a singular purpose:

> Under five minutes, we're not going to hold it for the last shot, but we're going to control the tempo. We're going to let them make the mistakes and we're going to become more deliberate, take time off the clock, and get those high percentage shots. Under two, now we're going to the deep freeze. We're going to take a lay-up if we can get it and then we're going to play for the free throws. I stuck with that same philosophy from that point on and never changed.

> I was just watching the tape of when we beat Proviso East last year at the Proviso West tournament. They went up one with maybe 35 seconds or so, a lot of guys would call time-out and set up a play; I don't believe in that, not when you have the right people in there. Because when you call time 1) you've got to get the ball in bounds; 2) you allow your opponent to adjust his defense. So, we just held the ball. We spread the floor and held the ball and they eventually came after us; Evan penetrated and passed to Garrett Leffleman underneath for the win. (Gene)

The Practice Session: Details, Details

John Wooden often commented about the sanctity of the practice session, the importance of the design of the plan, and the inclusion of the most fundamental details such as putting your socks on properly to avoid blisters. He regretted that the general public was unable to see the fastest and most powerful players in the nation compete against each other in no-dribble games and other intense drills. Most successful retired coaches acknowledge that the practice session is what they miss most:

> No matter how bad the season may be, I come to practice every day enthused and ready to go until they do something. Do you

know what I mean? I don't come to the practice moping like: "Hey, I don't want to be here." I come every day enthusiastic because I'm positive. I know we'll get the job done. We're going to win the next game.

This team [in February, 2008] might not be responding. So I get mad about it. So maybe I have to start backing off a little bit and start using some other players. Over the weekend, I was upset that we got beat and didn't compete the way I thought we should on Saturday. We've always gone there and done well [Batavia High School]. And then I start thinking: "You know, instead of coming in and going crazy on them on Monday, I'm going to talk to them. Look. We screwed up. We didn't compete. We have four games left. Three are conference and we can still win the conference and we can still do well in the state tournament that's coming up. We need to get together and just start playing." I'm talking to them. I don't know if it's going to work, but that's what I did. (Gene)

February is a tell-tale month for basketball teams. Coaches approach this month differently than the previous three because by this time they know what kind of cards they've been dealt for a possible post season run:

I felt that by February I was able to cut it back. Quality time instead of just keeping them. Shoot, before the girls came, my practices were three hours long. If I had a fault, even though I have a practice schedule, my coaches had to remind me, "Coach, we've got to move on." Because I would get carried away and I'm still like that. I wanted to get the job done and it would just take time. My big thing is that I would go over and over and over things. I try not to as much. I like to move on. My practices still move. We go from one thing to another without a lot of lollygagging. But what happens sometimes is that I'll stay with one thing too long if it's not going right and we'll still move on to everything else. (Gene)

Pingatore's relentless commitment to learning and achievement was refreshing in an educational society that pushes kids through the system often woefully under prepared. Achievement is hard and honest and rewarding. Achievement requires a teacher like Ping who battled uninspired learners to appreciate the detail laden ingredients that comprise success, no matter the time, space, disposition, or circumstance:

> The only difference now is I've got to get off the floor for the girls [St. Joseph merged with Immaculate Heart of Mary all-girls school in 2005]. So I feel my practices are sort of screwed up now. Like the little free throw game we play. You break up your team in three groups of five and everyone has got to make a free throw in their group. So for everyone you miss, you run a sprint and then you come back and try again until mastery. That whole group has got to stay until they make five consecutive free throws. Well, you're putting kids under pressure and they're putting their partners under pressure because they made it. It works. It really works. (Gene)

The voice of a coach is his most valuable instrument. Most coaches abuse their voices beyond repair, recognize the abuse, and eventually strategize to protect them. But some drills and some situations require full decibel amplification. Gene described one of those drills that had stressed his vocal chords:

> I do a full court drill every day of the year and I've been doing it a long time. My voice couldn't handle it. I picked it up after listening to Ernie Kivisto saying how he does 3 on 3 and you've got to score in 4 seconds. But when I did it, I made them score in 4 seconds back and forth. That's when Dennis Doyle use to

say to me: "You've got to get them off the court. You're going to kill them." Well, you want to kill them. I'm going to tell you what. I would say that that's the #1 reason why that by the end of the season, we were wearing people down in the fourth quarter because of that drill. We were in better shape because of that drill. The kids don't even realize it. They don't know what we're doing. They think that we're punishing them or whatever. I do it. I love it. (Gene)

Communication: Critical Conversations

As you may have noticed in this narrative data, Gene used rhetorical questions in conversation. I admit that early in the interview, I would attempt to answer his questions, but he would answer them quicker than I was able. I assumed my slow brain was boring him until he gleefully divulged one of his techniques to engage his students. "How about this? One of my favorite phrases is: 'When I ask you a question, I don't want an answer! [Laughter] I'm asking, but I really don't want an answer.'" He was constantly searching for avenues to connect to his students' brains and had mastered differentiated instruction. He shared frustration with technological advancement in this story.

During a time out, we laid out the plan: "If they score right now, you've got to hit them with the press." They scored and knocked the lead down to 7. What do you think my guys did? They turned around and picked up at half court. I'm livid! What the hell is this? So I vented about that to some of the teachers at school. They told me: "You know you have to understand something. Ever since we have been a 100% laptop school at St. Joe's [which was in the 3rd year], we as teachers find it very difficult to lecture the kids anymore. They don't pay attention. They're so used to a laptop where they can do it themselves and we see it every day. So you've got them in the huddle and they probably didn't pay attention. They're not used to it." What do I have to do? When I call a huddle, do

I have to e-mail each of them? Or it's something visual. I'm going to end up writing 4X PRESS, go get 'em on the grease board. What the hell? (Gene)

Ping always succeeded in communicating with kids. Simply, he cared about them and they cared about him. He peppered his conversations with motivating stories, current events, and even some fiction:

I'll bring up stuff in the paper where so and so said this or: "We're not rated anymore guys!" I mean there is all kinds of stuff. Yeah. The psychology, I'm constantly talking. If they're going to play against a certain kid, I might even lie a little bit you know? This kid said he's going to kick your ass! That's old school stuff. I talk more about our former players doing great or bad and use these guys as examples. Watch Illinois. Do you see Demitri? He's playing really good. (Gene)

But, where Coach Pingatore excelled was in his ability to confront students honestly about their present and future challenges:

I started with Isiah. I'll never forget the conservations with him: I know you're not challenged, but you're the leader and the way you play is the way they're going to play. So you've got to come on and bust your ass and that's what he did. And I've had those conversations with all these kids. They're the right kind of kids. If they weren't, they wouldn't be in the program. If they weren't, they'd be weeded out by freshman coach Hornacek and the guys in the lower level. (Gene)

Statistics: Numbers are Limiting

Statistics keeping and analysis are a part of every sport; however, Coach Pingatore had his own view on this:

I do stats and I don't...I eventually put them up after the games. We don't dwell on them. I look at a lot of the team stuff,

> like team free-throw stuff and rebound stuff to show them that
> if we had made our free-throws we would have had this game.
> Otherwise, I'm not huge on stats. (Gene)

Unlike the old days, avid players have access to multiple resources to learn the game. AAU, private coaches, fitness specialists, parents, street agents, college coaches, internet sites, and peers all bring varying perspectives to young, hungry, and impressionable players. Like other high school coaches, Gene became frustrated when players did not retain critical program knowledge:

> That's one of the most challenging things that has happened.
> When we had them in the summer, they didn't go to that
> stuff (AAU). They were with me. As a player, if I'm teaching
> them this and now they're going to come back to me after the
> summer, are they going to have the habit that I taught them?
> It's very difficult. Now, with the AAU culture, they lose it.
> They're not going to have it, so I start all over. That's the biggest
> thing today that I feel is a problem is when we start practice,
> we virtually…no matter what I taught them a year ago, we're
> starting all over. (Gene)

Relationships: They're Like My Own Kids

The day following Gene Pingatore's 800th victory, the *Chicago Tribune's* Doug Hammer wrote a brief summary of the victory over Carmel and the journey the Chargers began in 1969 when "Ping" assumed the reigns of this now legendary program. In that same sports section there were mentions of Iowa University (home of Tory Freeman Jr.), Notre Dame University (home of Jonathon Peoples), Ohio State University (home of Evan Turner), the New York Knicks (home of Isiah Thomas), and University of Illinois (home of Demetri McCarny). With one scan of a newspaper on Saturday, December 15, 2007, the power of "Ping" didn't need 6 degrees of separation. He capped the *Tribune* article with words that revealed what mattered most to this high school hoops hero: "It's not about me. It's about the multitude of players and coaches who contribute. We've created a neat program here. It's more than just basketball. We've become a family."

Gene's face glowed whenever he spoke of his players, coaches, and their families. He received countless calls, sometimes for help late in the evening, sometimes to bail parents of his players out of jail, sometimes to escort his players and former players away from dangerous places, but most times, alums called him for advice or just to check in. Pingatore would do what he could for his players because they were his kids:

> I love the camaraderie of it and the people. They were all part of it. So, yes, that makes it special. But as far as working hard and doing the best you can, I'm going to do that in whatever I do. I just don't believe you can do it any other way. So, if I'm working at my job at school, I'm doing that the best way I can and enjoying it. If I've not enjoyed it, I'll get out of it and I won't do it. I enjoyed the basketball because I get a charge out of seeing the success of the kids. I get a charge out of seeing them do well in college. I get a charge out of them becoming bigwigs in whatever they do. I mean you have that. These were all guys who were part of my life and they're like my own kids. That's the way I look at it. Of course, there were some more than others.

> They're like my family. How do you abandon those kids? You can't. I'll never forget. I get my whole family involved. I'll never forget. And you know what? It never ends. It doesn't end when your players graduate. You have them forever...forever. You'll get a call out of the blue and now what? Jesus Chriminy. Now what? I give them a hard time about it all. That's just my way, but then I do it. I help them. The other thing is you've got to do that stuff. Otherwise, when you're talking about the whole thing as just about wins and losses, what the hell was that?

I sort of alluded to it when my 800th came out, but I think it's more than treating the whole thing as wins and losses. They become part of our basketball family. When they were part of it, I think they knew that the coaches in the program cared about them, were there for them, and were there for them after they were gone.

The caring thing is really important and the college thing is important, not just Division I. The fact that anyone that plays, if they feel like they want to go somewhere and play Division III, we're going to make a call for them; we're going to get them into play, and help them go to school. In '87, that was a loaded team. We took 3rd in state. It was Scales, Mister, Molis and I remember that another group came off the bench featuring Carl Hayes. The next year they and Deryl Cunningham were big time.

I'm always conscious of doing that kind of thing, of calling kids in and going over stuff. Today, I did it with Diamond. I called him in and said: "Diamond, you can't do what you did. You've got to be ready to play. You know you've got to work on that mid-range game. Are you watching television?" Did you see Demitri? He's always going to the basket. He gets every shot blocked. You've got to stop. You can't constantly do stuff like that. Hopefully, somewhere along the line it's going to sink in. Not just for us…. That's for him! Because he can get away with the play he's doing in high school, but he's not going to get away with it in college. I'm really concerned about those kids that are moving on to play. I want them to be successful. (Gene)

In January 2011, Coach Gene Pingatore became the winningest coach in the history of Illinois Basketball. Above all else, his formula for success was captured in the paragraph above and his commitment and drive was captured in the words: "I want them to be successful."

CHAPTER SIX

●

STEVE PAPPAS:
GORDON TECH AND DEERFIELD HIGH SCHOOLS
"I am a part of all that I have met"
~Tennyson from *Ulysses*

June 2006

The nurses were affected. As Steve's final battle with cancer caused his chemo ravaged body to porously bleed out, the businesslike nurses who witnessed thousands of hideous deaths in this cancer ICU ward at Northwestern Memorial Hospital in Chicago were deeply and hysterically wounded. Their visceral response to his loss moved me. They had battled alongside Steve and his loyal spouse Cathie for months. They understood and valued his rarity. They wept.

Steve spent most of his adult life inspiring those people around him to "get it"—*embrace the opportunities available to us while being strong teammates for one another.* On June 8, 2006, the Chicago educational community lost one of its finest sons. Legendary teacher, hall of fame coach, and school leader, Steve Pappas courageously accepted his ultimate defeat to an insidiously persistent non-Hodgkin's Lymphoma after a two and one half year battle. He was fifty-four. Steve influenced the lives of thousands of Deerfield High School, Gordon Tech High School, and St. Demetrios Grade School students and colleagues who were privileged to share ideas about life, literature, and philosophy. Whether these lessons occurred in classrooms, playing fields, or basketball courts, his profound love for mankind, which fueled Steve's hopeful approach to life, rang true and bountiful. Steve held many positions in his short life: husband, son, brother, friend, mentor, teacher, coach, department chair, leader, and student; but what separated him from others was his foundational confidence that people were *kind* and that life provided invitations to all of us to share our kindness. I'm sickened by the thought that I'll never again hear Steve's wise and distinctively hopeful voice remind us that life is TEAM FIRST.

Early Years: Albany Park, Chicago

The adventures of young Steve Pappas were headquartered in River Park, a meandering acreage designed in classic Chicago Park District style along the banks of the North Branch of the Chicago River on Foster Avenue. As a boy, Steve was always in search of a game. Baseball was his first love, but football, tennis, and eventually basketball filled his days and nights with countless situations, angles, conflicts, and learning opportunities. Late in his life, Steve would often mourn the fact that unsupervised play and all of its life preparing lessons on the sandlots of America all but evaporated when double income lifestyles became the norm. The older boys welcomed young Steve into their games. In turn, Steve shared his experiential knowledge with his peers. Most of us who coached with or against Steve agree that he was born with an innate proclivity to inspire and lead others toward a common goal, but these experiences at River Park, St. Demetrios, and other play-lots throughout ethnically diverse Chicago clarified his evolving philosophy of sport.

Other friends recalled Steve's ability to play through pain, his athletic dominance in whatever sport he chose, and most frequently, his magnetism. Everyone wanted to play on Steve's team. They knew that his teams succeeded and enjoyed themselves while doing so. He would invite friends to "go on a run," meaning go to the local park (Loyola, Margate, Angel Guardian, etc.) and dominate the basketball court. In pick-up games, a team stays on the court until it is defeated. Steve's teams rarely left the court. They went on runs. Opponents had to double and triple team Steve because of his quickness, vision, and uncanny knack for scoring and playmaking. Consequently, he rarely scored. Instead, he read situations, drew opponents near, and set his teammates up for the spoils of scoring success. His former teammates recalled the confident grin he flashed when delivering the shooter a pin-point accurate and cleverly crafted assist. The grin communicated victory and his complete belief that the shooter had nothing to think about except his follow through. That sophisticated level of gamesmanship inspired everyone to want to be on Steve's teams. Dennis Zelasko, storied coach and dear friend said, "He had a great knack of knowing what people needed from him. It wasn't like he was my best friend; he was everybody's best friend."

Family: Working Parents

Steve Pappas grew up in a tiny bungalow a block away from St. Demetrios Church. He and his younger siblings, Jimmy and Nancy, were raised by working parents. Eddy, Steve's father, owned The Olive Branch—a hard core tavern on the North Side of Chicago. Eddy was rarely home, which accelerated Steve's maturity. Some kids would stray into nefarious activities when granted the level of Steve's independence. In typical Pappas form, Steve flourished in his freedom, kept adequate grades in school, but began to build a career through his fascination with competitive sport.

Steve's wife, Cathie, provided context for his decision to pursue his master's degree:

> Education was not a value that came from his home. Whether you became something or didn't become something, you worked and you paid your bills, and that was fine. But there was always something in Steve that wanted more than that. Steve picked up in unusual ways, which makes me honor even more who he was because he had to do it in ways that were difficult. I mean there was no financial support. There was no emotional support. There were no educated role models. There were models that were tough models, in fact. Steve would often reflect that some of the patterns in his home he had to guard against. I think some of his greatest fear was about not letting that become his personality. And I think some of it did

become who he was. Early on at Gordon, there was a moment
when he just had had enough of what he was, and the madness
around him, and that's when he knew he had to get out of town
and ended up in Oregon. Oregon was a state of peace that
Steve loved. (Cathie Pappas)

Steve revered his mother, Hazel. Her kind warmth and old-world wisdom
were qualities he acquired through the many challenges they faced together in
stabilizing the household. Steve religiously met Hazel each evening after her
late shift at the local Sears and Roebuck. He scheduled his own employment,
classes, and practices around her work schedule in order to drive her home
each evening. In serving Hazel, he never wavered:

Many of Steve's charismatic qualities were influenced by his mother's
example.

He could deal with his home life, but he knew his mother
couldn't and so he became his mother's protector, his mother's,
you know, go-to person. He talked about his mother in such
a way, with such love and appreciation, that it was a very
important piece that he wanted me to understand. Not about
the tough stuff at home, but just about her, how, and I see
some of this in Steve; she always had a smile no matter what
the situation was. And he talked about that smile and how
important it was and how hard she worked for the family
because dad wasn't bringing in enough money. She had an
incredible knack of making friends; friends that really were
good people; again, much like Steve. People mattered. She
sold washing machines and did such a good job at it that they
moved her up to this or that. But sales were her thing and
she really enjoyed her work and her relationships at Sears.
(Cathie Pappas)

Another adult that shaped Steve's life was his hard-on-his-luck uncle Ted. Ted was Hazel's alcoholic brother. Eddy reluctantly granted Ted a place in the basement. Ted was not allowed upstairs, but Steve spent hours wiling away with Ted and their mutual affinity for the history of baseball down in the dank basement on Winnemac Street in Chicago. I am convinced that this odd but critical relationship with Ted taught young Steve about individual differences and disabilities, which may account for his overwhelming kindness, particularly for underdogs as well as his advocacy for the inclusion of the marginalized. I have yet to meet a more accessible human being.

Becoming a Coach: Steve's DNA

Steve Pappas was one of the most celebrated athletes in Mather High School history. Baseball, basketball, and football were his focus. Academic achievement had not yet resonated. In the summer of his junior year, Steve realized that physically and athletically his football team could compete, but recognized that his inexperienced and perhaps disinterested coaches would be unable to provide an acceptable system of play. One of Steve's prized possessions was a framed, full page personal response from legendary Alabama football coach Bear Bryant. Steve wrote Coach Bryant explaining the challenge and within weeks, received the *Alabama Football Playbook* and kind words from the "Bear" about Steve's moxie and commitment to learning. This type of initiative and creative problem solving served Steve well through high school as well as his storied career at Grand Canyon College in Arizona.

After leading the NAIA National Champions at Grand Canyon College, Steve considered an offer to play professionally in Greece. He chose instead to begin a career in coaching and St. Demetrios Grade School became his internship. Today, those former St. Demetrios players are now some of Chicago's most successful doctors, teachers, accountants, and CEO's. All of them point to an occasion when an angry Steve Pappas marched down from the bleachers, entered their locker room after an embarrassing loss to the perennial Greek basketball powerhouse from Palos Hills. Steve, who was not their coach, demanded from that moment forward they prepare for next spring's tournament and a rematch. He committed himself to them and they somehow, under his guidance, defeated their heavily favored south side nemesis. To a man, they spoke of Steve's belief in them and this life lesson in overcoming odds was at the core of their collective success. Each of these men courageously battled to save their beloved coach from the claws of cancer. The lifelong relationships they shared with each other and with Steve were authentic and inspiring.

How I Met Steve Pappas
December 1983

I fought all the freakish ugliness of the Dan Ryan Expressway during its rush hour on a blustery, lake effect snow blown, dark, December game night. Rushing out of the heat of varsity basketball practice at Fenwick High School in homey Oak Park, inhaling a Maxwell Street Polish, fries, and a pop, while negotiating impatient motorists and the uncooperative folds of my Chicago street finder map, I sped toward 101st and Ewing, someplace near Hegewich, under the Skyway on the Southeast Side.

The stench of laboring steel mills commingling with the pungency of grilled onions assaulted my nostrils as I weaved through the gritty street configurations blanketed by yellow neon light in search of Catholic League power, St. Francis de Sales. Chicago's south side rarely exudes welcoming warmth, but the snow removed and protected parking spaces adorned with beaten up chairs and old broomsticks punctuated its territorial toughness. After 90 minutes commuting in my unheated Ford Pinto, I sprinted four blocks to the gym, past the ticket lines, flashed my scout credentials, and vaulted to the balcony to learn what I could about the sophomore and varsity cagers of Gordon Tech High School, next week's opponent and tonight's scouting report focus.

This was a typical Friday night in the life of an assistant coach in Chicago's hotbed of basketball—40 plus hours a week for a five hundred dollar annual stipend beyond one's classroom responsibilities as a teacher, which helped pay the bills. We worked cheap because coaching secured our positions. The only reason we were hired over teachers with better academic credentials was because of our abilities as coaches and recruiters. My goal was to help build the program, to help my boss climb, thus opening a position for me to pursue the opportunity of running my own show. We were afforded few alternatives. Out work, out smart, out hustle, out class, and ultimately out recruit our opponents. Win championships and capture the imagination of potential recruits and their parents. Driving through the south side, pondering its distinctively diverse enclaves affirmed my curiosity about this desperate game. I loved its intensity and competitiveness, yet understood it was hijacking my life. Basketball truly is the city game. Pile on the recruiting turf battles and the city game becomes the city war. When we weren't scouting, we were practicing, weight lifting, evaluating grade school players, organizing grade school showcase tournaments and camps, or visiting with college coaches hoping to ascend to the next level. One thing we didn't do was fraternize with the opponent. Not only did we not have time, but competition for prominence was fierce and everything but friendly. One losing season could cost your job. Several losing seasons could close a school.

We were all aware of the Catholic League coaching legends: Dick Versace—Gordon Tech, to Bradley U., to the NBA; Tony Barone—Mt. Carmel, to Creighton U., to the NBA. If we could offer something special, these opportunities may become ours. Hundreds of coaches clung to these examples and in most cases all but extinguished their family lives and teaching careers while chasing these insane dreams. The urgency was simply too great! To make your name, you needed first to win and win big. Ethics were often lost.

Gordon Tech's varsity was seated in the balcony; their coaches clad in designer suits perched above the players in the top rows. I knew them because my boss, Will Rey, to this day one of the most complete educators in the game, had recently left their staff to assume head coach responsibilities at Crete Monee and now Fenwick High School. Awkwardly, I approached them and said hello. They kindly nodded and returned their gazes to the game below. Amidst the seated players, not sitting with his fellow coaches, was assistant coach, Steve Pappas. His long hair, faded green canvas Army coat, frayed pants cuffs, and scuffed Thom McAns contrasted starkly with the attire of his colleagues. He stood up, as if to greet someone of prominence. That someone was me. He lauded me for my work with Coach Rey at Fenwick and invited me to sit with him and the team while I scouted the sophomore game. This snapshot summarizes my first encounter with Steve Pappas. Anyone who knew him marveled at his ability to make people feel important. I learned the first of many Pappas lessons of leadership that evening. Little did I know, I gained a friend, colleague, mentor, and a kinship that would grow in mutual respect through the next twenty-three years. The world misses Coach Pappas. I miss my brother.

Chicago high school basketball during the 1980s slugged through gang affiliation, high school and college recruiting wars, racism, shoe contracts, street agents, drugs and alcohol, violence, yet most of all, passionate dominance. Any Friday night, heated battles were waged in band box gyms all over Chicago. The culture was brash and cut throat.

Steve never really fit. His closest friends vowed that he led a charmed existence, and that everything he touched turned to gold. He enjoyed our company, but his perceptive nature coupled with his acute understanding of relationship and teamwork accelerated him beyond us to brilliance.

Baptism by Fire

Steve's brilliance and the strength of his coaching was his uncanny ability to maintain balance, especially in times of turmoil. He could fire up a team better than anyone, yet at the risk of sounding mystical, was balanced by his wonderful sense of recognizing all the forces at play. While we scurried like fighting rats to gain an edge, Steve mindfully and patiently sought thoughtful ways to inspire his students and staff to, as he would say, "get it."

The great game of basketball was an instrument to help build strong, powerful, and dignified men. Why waste this beautiful game chasing victories?

Former colleague and roommate, Karl Costello, marveled at Steve's harmony with the world. Karl and Steve cut their teeth as teachers and coaches at Gordon Tech High School. Costello suggested that Pappas possessed extraordinary intuitive qualities as articulated by public leadership guru, Ronald Heifetz, through his metaphor which described the perspectives and relationship between the dance floor and the balcony. Steve's first encounter coaching a varsity squad revealed his ability to enjoy the dance, move harmoniously with the other dancers, and appreciate the intimacy of the music on the dance floor; but what distinguished young Coach Pappas was his savant-like ability to view the action from the balcony and understand its movements, providing him with uncanny insight and a decided advantage. Karl Costello shared a story that highlighted this gift:

> I'll never forget Steve's response when Bob's [Bob Ociepka, Gordon Tech's former Head Coach] mother died and we [young assistant coaches] were left in charge of the team. We're at Leo High School and because Bob wasn't there and his presence was so strong with the team, I was anxious and curious about how the players would respond to us. It was interesting to see their eyes. You know, then there was the aura of: We've gotta win this one for Coach. But no one talked about that. No one said that. So, in the pregame classroom, they needed to have something that was different, not in like the opposite of Bob, but different in maybe a newer type of focus. It was different in the how. But there was still the Steve Pappas edge. There still was some humor; there still was some seriousness, but it was just low-key because Steve himself knew that the kids were already wound up. He was extraordinarily calm, like he'd done this before.

> We're losing the game in the first half. And his half-time talk was all about the task at hand, the sense of purpose; not we've gotta win one for the "Gipper." If I would have been in his shoes, I could have seen myself out of earshot of the kids turning to Steve and going: "We can't go back to Gordon without bringing this one home." But he didn't say that to me and there wasn't even like, like a look. It was this calm, this

balance, and then we went out and we kicked their ass in the second half and we won the game!

It wasn't just one thing though; it was like everything was connected. It was like the whole…the bus ride, the pre-game talk was probably the beginning. We rode the buses before. With JV games, there were times when maybe Ociepka wasn't on the bus but never in the locker room, dressed in uniform before the game. Now we're gonna go out and warm up and play. From that moment on, until the very end of the game, we had a calm sense of purpose. We had some wild celebrations with those Gordon teams, but that was the wildest. It was maybe the most fulfilling celebration at the end. The kids took Steve's lead. They earned an important victory for the program, period. (Karl Costello)

Well-Rounded Education
The following school year, Steve disrupted the momentum of his teaching and coaching career, took an unpaid sabbatical from Gordon Tech, loaded up his car, and took off for Lewis and Clark College, one of two schools in the nation that allowed Steve to earn his master's degree in one year:

That is Steve. Another example, like who picks up and goes to Lewis and Clark College in Bumblefuck, Oregon and takes a sabbatical, okay? The rest of us conventionally chipped away evenings for many years to knock out a master's. Not Steve. He worked nights in the paper mill and somehow kept up with his books, never once looking back or doubting his plan. (Karl Costello)

Two years later, in 1986, Steve applied for the head coach position at Gordon and impressed the search committee with his global vision of educating men. His portfolio and credentials included concepts from Gandhi, Lincoln, and

Homer. The other candidates came armed with binders filled with X's and O's. Steve was named head coach at Gordon Tech, promised to improve an already formidable program, and quickly built one of the most competitive programs in Illinois. Conference, regional, and sectional championships as well as a run at the state championship in 1989 propelled Steve into the media limelight and the top of Chicago high school hoops. Erin's Glen, a local tavern on Montrose Avenue, posted "Give Coach Pappas a Raise" on its outdoor marquee. Three coach of the year awards later and Steve, forever the student, recognized that life was comfortable, too comfortable. Again, he took a long stride into the unknown and accepted a teaching and coaching position at Deerfield High School, a proud school renowned for everything excellent, except basketball. Coach Pappas rolled up his sleeves.

First Date: A Need for Change

When Steve left Gordon for Deerfield in 1992, he also exchanged his life for a radically different routine. Much like Shakespeare's Henry, Steve put aside the late night excesses, focused inward, and sought refuge in the teachings of Christ. Cathie Pappas, Steve's widow, recollected Steve's state of mind prior to leaving Gordon Tech:

> He said he was lying in bed in his apartment in Ravenswood, thinking about his life and where it was. The madness surrounded him. He said I can't do this on my own. I can't do this on my own. He said the minute he surrendered the control over, everything started differently and he would remind me of that. (Cathie Pappas)

He also met Cathie Childs, the love of his life. These two "teammates" charted a new path together. Their first date was a trip to Steve's humble origins. He explained his "gym rat" life in the dark facility at St. Demetrios. They walked the play fields at River Park and visited his room on Winnemac Ave. replete with the hundreds of sports stickers adorning any available furniture surface or wall space. It appeared that Steve wanted Cathie to see him completely:

I was just incredibly touched that he would share so much of his life. I mean I was honored. He was very kind and he was very good, I think, in helping me understand the pieces that were important and valued in his life. He did that really well. So we didn't even go to a movie or anything. Hopped in the car and went from one spot to another. End of story. (Cathie Pappas)

Steve Pappas was one of those rare high school coaches who loved teaching English as much as teaching the great game of basketball. He valued the power of ideas and was in constant search of a new lesson usually inspired by a story. Of Steve's many gifts, his ability to deliver a crystal clear lesson through story telling will be the gift that keeps Steve alive in all of us. He quoted from countless passages of literature. *Ulysses* by Tennyson is a poem that not only influenced the manner in which Steve approached life, but also captured the essence of Steve. Ulysses was a natural leader, champion sportsman, and loyal man of integrity, just like Steve. "I am a part of all that I have met," is a line from *Ulysses* that Steve wove into his personal philosophy. He sought interesting people, folks on the fringes, "ordinary Joes" with extraordinary stories. Other coaches cozied up to power brokers that could help advance their careers. Steve reached out to the eccentrics and the genuine. He, like Ulysses, understood the importance of companionship, especially when on a journey to the unknown, and Steve was always on a journey. Minerva, Goddess of Wisdom, chided Ulysses for entrusting his journey to the colorful misfits with whom he travelled. Ulysses didn't see the short-comings of his crew members; he chose instead to celebrate their strengths. Frequently, this caused set -backs, but just as frequently inspired remarkable adventures worth telling for generations. We were Steve's crew of colorful misfits. He loved us, inspired us, nudged us, and treasured our stories. Ulysses had nothing on Steve Pappas.

"I Am a Part of All That I Have Met"

Cathie Pappas, Steve's wife and teaching partner, witnessed first- hand the Pappas methods of education, the first of which is, *I can't teach you until I can reach you*:

> Kids felt that their best friend at Deerfield High School was Steve Pappas. There are so many kids who didn't know I was present when they were making comments about Steve. I was always taken by the fact, hoping kids were making the same kind of comments about me. I thought, wow, maybe just one! But they were always from the toughest kids able to say, "I love him." They didn't say, "It was a great class." But first they said how much they loved him and they did it without any reservation. These are tough guys with other tough guys making these kinds of comments. And Steve had that capacity to make us all feel better about who we were and we loved him for that.
>
> Steve excelled with kids off the beaten path. He would introduce ideas respectfully: "You know there's a little diversion here and I really want you guys to hear how Homer wrote this without any of the editing that took place." And they kind of liked that. He did that in a nice way. He used films. Steve had a wonderful way, especially with the average kids, of involving, showing something, reading something, showing something, talking about something, writing about it. But his classroom had many facets to it and I think that's true of his coaching.
>
> He pulled in a lot of different directions, a lot of different types and forms of ways to help people enter the discourse; like maybe I enter best through this media and you enter best through that. And he was such a master in doing it in a seamless way. He did it for the sake of enjoyment, not

consciously saying well there are certain kids that learn this way, certain kids that learn that way. He did it because he felt it's such a fun and interesting way to study. Bring in the history; bring in the art; bring in the film; bring in the original text; bring in something that his professor had written to him during the study of *The Odyssey*. He was constantly collecting artifacts to engage people. (Cathie Pappas)

According to educator, Stephanie Pace Marshall, "How we engage the minds of our children in learning profoundly shapes the patterns of their thinking and their thinking shapes the world." Coach Pappas differentiated instruction to engage multiple intelligences in a manner consistent with Dewey, Goleman, Marshall, and Marzano, but his delivery and methodology was natural and unrehearsed. Daniel Pink implored the value of this type of teaching and learning, "People who hope to thrive in the Conceptual Age must understand the connections between diverse and seemingly separate disciplines." Steve's quest for the spiritual guided Steve's journey:

He read so much, so many articles, and would search them out dealing with the spiritual piece of all our selves. He was intrigued by it. He believed it was vital and so all of his binders were filled with all these passages that he had handwritten out from some spiritual piece that he had read, most often from the Bible. (Cathie Pappas)

Meet Kids Where They Are

Cathie Pappas drew on her own experience to explain how Steve met learners, and people in general, where they were.

That's exactly what he did with kids. I wanted to be a real athlete. I mean a real athlete. On one of our first dates I said, "I really want to learn how to play basketball, Steve. I never had a coach in my life. Could you just show me something?" So he said, "Throw the ball against the wall." I said, "What's that going to do?" He said, "It will show me what I have to work with." So then we did a few things and then he said, "Okay, we'll pick up with it [We have a baseline from which to begin]."

Looking at it later I realized how natural it was for him to enter into the learning process. He didn't say, "Are you kidding? Another day." He absolutely made me feel like, yeah, okay, and we'll see what we can do with this, and then I never stopped. It was like okay, can we do this tomorrow? And the thing was is that he allowed that. He allowed that. (Cathie Pappas)

Again, Coach Pappas exhibited his ease in scaffolding and pacing and engaging his student through a framework of motivation and relevance. Cathie described this as Steve "finding the spot":

So we're going up and down the court in the gym. I'd have him in there Sunday morning and I wasn't doing so good at these baskets. And he said, "You know what? I think this is your spot. This is your spot!" And it was the way he said it and the way he just kind of uplifted me to believe that it was coming along here. We found that spot. Every time I was in that spot. And it was the same in the classroom with kids. He was all the time kind of allowing you to feel your passion, your feelings, your...what it is you know about yourself. And then he would find the spot and, once he found the spot, kids began to feel that success and it just has a contagious kind of feel about it. And he was just so good at that. (Cathie Pappas)

Coach Pappas celebrated individuality in his students and enjoyed the challenge of meshing personalities while stirring imagination, collaboration, and creativity through problem solving:

Coach allowed personality, all your idiosyncrasies, to just kind of play out there like a good teacher would and he's assessing and using the capacity that he was so good at in kind of just looking at this and figuring out how am I going to make this work? And he always found the spot, and that was the same in the classroom. And this was I think beautiful about him. He never tried to remake you or make you. He simply would believe in what you were believing in, whatever that piece was about yourself, and then use that to keep the momentum. I think it was a fascinating piece. Steve never tried to control a classroom. I mean he was always in complete control but he never tried to control a classroom. He let it be spontaneous. (Cathie Pappas)

In *The Quality School*, Glasser wrote passionately about the spontaneous freedom necessary for genuine education. Coach Pappas led students to learning not through coercion but through fascination and the human desire to learn:

Honestly. That's it. The genuineness of it. And you loved him for that. That's why the kids loved him. That's why I loved him because you didn't have to be something else. It was like, you know what, we're all just broken. (Cathie Pappas)

Important Conversations

For Steve, the "classroom" was anywhere and everywhere he would encounter students and he created informal opportunities to let them know that what they had to say was important to him:

He had ongoing conversations with kids about who they were and what they wanted to be, and he was such a good listener. And he valued those conversations. I mean he really made time for those conversations. Those sound like things that come easy in a class or in a school day and they're not.

He was so available in the morning before school and it would always just look like he was there with his cup of coffee. Always telling kids, "I'll see you tomorrow morning. I'm going to be here." And those conversations would take place. And for the kids at risk, you could just see how important it was to have the special attention of one human being in that school and what it did for them. After school was the basketball stuff, but in the morning he'd be there and interesting enough these kids would show up and be invested in those conversations. And then ongoing, "Coach, you got a minute tomorrow?" That kind of thing. (Cathie Pappas)

Steve Pappas created strategies to ignite students' passions while complying with administrative mandates. He found middle ground, kept his eye on the ball, and rarely if ever shortchanged his students' access to his remarkable brain and soul:

Steve also had a lot of hard conversations with kids and with basketball players. I mean sometimes I'd see kids return with their faces beet red. He would have the capacity to do that. He'd always begin a year with: What does it look like for you? Let's talk about it. And he would expose his own self on that. I think Steve with the idea of dreams, big dreams made good teams. He really believed that about people. Listening to the dream, respecting it, and affirming it. I was always appreciative of how transparent he was. Steve was always who he was. And not from like the important coach in the building, but from a human being who had done some good stuff and not so good stuff and listen to the story because you might not want to follow those footsteps. But he was very, very transparent. And I don't think often as a teacher we feel we want to take that risk. He was never their buddy, but they knew he was genuine. And he didn't have to be whole. He didn't have to be perfect and for some reason the kids made him perfect but he…His conversations about his own learning were never like that. He talked about his writing one time with kids: "I never did very much writing as a kid, never asked to do very much writing, never prodded to do it, but once I got started I couldn't stop." (Cathie Pappas)

Hope and Confidence

"This is us" and "this is not us" were phrases and a tool to remind students about the philosophical underpinnings of Deerfield basketball employed by Coach Pappas. He constantly provided examples of basic human behavior that would either live "with us" or "not with us." Respect for others was at the foundation of his philosophy. When players were knocked down, Steve honored them for getting up immediately and enthusiastically. He demanded his squad to pick each other and opponents up whenever they fell. Steve periodically would refer to legendary boxers Tommy Hearns and Ray Leonard to illuminate for players that life and competition is about giving hits, but more importantly, taking hits, being resilient, and keeping your wits about you:

> Steve would say that kids will live up to our expectations; the thing is we need clear expectations. When he got sick [cancer] and he had conversations with the kids about what he had hoped the room would be like when he wasn't there and there would be a permanent sub. But the clarity that he spoke about those expectations with a way that I also heard him talk about basketball and that sense that you will live up to this. For all the softness in Steve, there was that real clear piece that almost can move into I don't want to say hardness but a straight-forwardness and we're not going to tamper with this piece. We are not going to tamper with this piece. He was very good at that. Constant change is good and his classroom looked like that. He was never one to get into a long-term pattern. He enjoyed spontaneity. He enjoyed changes. He welcomed

transitions. And he would talk those out loud to help the kids look at what's going on. Humility, humbleness, kindness were things he always talked to the kids about through maybe a story that we were reading, through life pieces, but they seemed to be the three virtues that he really keyed on.

Steve tried to create places of excellence and passion in the classroom. There was the sense that flaws are a part of that, mistakes are a part of that, weakness is a part of that; that those things aren't separate from excellence and passion. And I think what that gave people is a sense of security to try. To experience, to try, and to honor that. He was huge on service and always took opportunities to talk about that element and its connectedness to leadership and how he saw that in a classroom and in the larger school community. (Cathie Pappas)

Humor helps to invite students out of their comfort zones and into a place where reaching, trying, and risking can elevate them to new growth:

There were always smiles and laughter going on in Steve's class. I mean always. And I'm sure we all want to bottle that, but kids wanted to be where they were because once you were a Steve Pappas kid or a part of that team you felt incredibly protected and with that came a sense of responsibility.

He ran quick-paced classrooms. For dealing with students who might have a difficult time processing, he ran very quick classrooms, much quicker than the pace of mine. Always prepare for sudden change. I mean it was going and they relished it. There was that constant push. At Gordon Tech, Steve seemed to have an incredible appreciation for the struggle those kids went through to be at Gordon Tech;

what that meant for the sacrifice; and had the ability to kind of transfer that appreciation to the kids without making them feel like a patronizing kind of thing or a victimization but to use it almost as a leverage that we're going to sail. We're moving on. (Cathie Pappas)

> *"It is how the teacher speaks to and behaves with the student that communicates respect and acceptance." (Marzano & Pickering)*

Honor People: Acknowledging Community

Steve exuded kindness and respect. I've witnessed coaches who lose track of these simple yet critical virtues, and unfortunately, their players soon lose track as well. An unraveling of the community ensues, making it all but impossible to grow:

He would honor the maintenance guys when they would come in the classroom or one of the runners that delivered nurses notes; he always called them by name and acknowledged the moment. It was like Steve was making a point of who that person is and what that person does, and kind of making everybody feel good about them. Steve particularly respected the custodians. He said to his students, "You know the guy that picks up your mess? That guy is my friend and I don't have my friends come in and pick up after anybody." And he did the same thing with the team and the bus and how it was going to be left. Every single person in that community has a role and a position and we need to look at that and acknowledge it. He was so good.

I remember him asking often that we look at the anger issue with troubled kids and his feeling was is that behind that anger are probably the real issues going on in that student's life and the anger is probably a masking of what the real problems might be. (Cathie Pappas)

Retired teachers and coaches lament the loss of their audience, the loss of their pulpit to stir ideas in a forum. Even in casual conversation, we learned from Steve. He relished the exchange of passionate ideas:

> People define Steve as being a good coach. Steve was a great teacher. They're one and the same and I'm sure that one just fed the other. But I do know that given the extraordinary situations that he was given at the end, his choice was to get back in that classroom and to teach. Every single meeting that we had with Dr. Gordon [oncologist] was about: When am I…I'm going back tomorrow? That's where I'm headed? It kept making me think about my own teaching and my love for my teaching. He really loved being a teacher. Steve really, really found great pleasure. I'm so glad that he did. That's exactly where he wanted to be, even to the bitter end. When I think of his leaving on May 24th, he had finished with the seniors that day. We all thought he was…I mean coming back. It was just closing the school year, but his goal was that year to finish out with the seniors. There was nowhere else he wanted to be. When you do it right like he did, the purpose of his being was all wrapped in that. You take that away from him, what's the purpose of his life, especially when you're fighting for your own life? That is your purpose.
>
> He was very encouraging to young teachers and others in the building. He was adamant about the gift of that job; the gift of that position; what can be done in a child's life, in a young person's life; what change can happen and to go for that ride and enjoy it. (Cathie Pappas)

Steve died two weeks later on June 8, 2006.

Man for Others

Steve acknowledged his friends with well-timed notes, calls, or gifts. He would organize impromptu meetings over a meal and cold beverages. We were honored by these invitations. In recognition of a strong season as coach of the St. Ignatius Wolfpack, Steve presented me with a plaque engraved with the words of Kipling, "The strength of the wolf is in the pack. The strength of the pack is in the wolf." The words are reflective of Steve's teaching philosophy, "All for one." He exhorted his teams and his friends to work together toward one common goal.

On an icy, sleet in your face Tuesday evening in December 1989, the upstart Wolfpack of St. Ignatius hosted undefeated and ranked Gordon Tech. Only the hoops faithful would brave such nasty weather to witness such a meaningless game. I was a young coach trying to prove to my team, the school, the Catholic League, and myself that I knew what I was doing. The Rams, led by Steve Pappas, were classic Gordon Tech in the image of those Versace and Ociepka teams: tough, smart, quick, and proud.

Steve's teams not only defended every inch of the floor, but they punished opponents physically and mentally due to their suffocating power, relentless work ethic, and tireless spirit. His kids recovered loose balls, took charges, dove for possessions, reached for rebounds, physically blocked out, ran their no dribble choreographed break, attacked the rim, and loved the game with an uncommon energy that distinguished them from their peers. They were gorgeous. Steve conducted these symphonic waves of joyful destruction. Teams like this are rare. Most lifer coaches never see a team like this. How did Steve Pappas produce these rare qualities in generations of players, year in and year out? "I can't take it anymore," one of my players said in the huddle.

"Are they dirty?" I asked.

"No, they're just good and they won't stop."

Great! How are we supposed to combat that combination?

But on this particular frigid evening on Roosevelt Road, we played in relative secrecy and disarmed the high octane Rams out of desperation by spreading to four corners and employing our center to dribble the ball up the floor versus their hellacious pressure. Somehow, some way, we prevailed. My players were stunned at the threshold they had crossed. The intellectuals of St. Ignatius College Prep had just defeated the Catholic League's most powerful squad. The arduous conditioning, monotonous drill work, taxing memorization, sweat, blood, and tears of frustration earned us a monumental and satisfying victory.

With mixed emotions, I watched the Gordon players and my friend, the usually upbeat coach, limp to the locker room, equally stunned and beginning to sort out the gravity of this embarrassing occurrence. Steve limped because of the debilitating psoriatic arthritis that inflated his knees to the size of cantaloupes and all but crippled him with searing pain throughout his life. The Gordon Tech players limped due to this blow to their collective hubris. Even at the high school level, parents, fans, writers, and sycophants will sting with their "limited picture" criticism. Steve had already begun formulating his strategy to heal the wounds inflicted during this secret skirmish.

The point of this story occurred fifteen minutes later, after Steve addressed his troops. As the Wolfpack jubilantly processed what had just transpired, my assistant explained that Coach Pappas was outside our locker room door and wished to speak to our team. Steve entered. Pain and exhaustion dominated his celebratory smile. He enthusiastically shook my hand and proceeded to demand that our young men recognize the magnitude of this event. He emphasized how disciplined, poised, and deserving we were while planting seeds in the players' heads about future conquests and building upon this notch in their collective belt. The faces of the players became hopeful and proud…and at that precise moment he explained to the Wolfpack how fortunate they were to have me as their coach. My credibility immediately sky rocketed in their eyes due to his selfless gesture.

In subsequent years, I learned that Steve periodically visited opponents' locker rooms after well played contests. Coach Pappas respected the lessons learned in competition. He recognized that worthy opponents inspired exceptional play. Rather than destroy competition, Steve chose to nurture excellence in adversaries to provide optimal challenges for his own teams. This acceptance of *All* into his life distinguished him from all but a handful of peers that understood the pure genius of Steve's motives. Above all, Steve Pappas committed to the betterment of mankind. Basketball was the vehicle.

The Brotherhood: Working Together for the Good

Working together in brotherhood became the creed for Steve and his teams at River Park, St. Demetrios, Mather, Mayfair, Grand Canyon, and Gordon Tech. When Steve recognized that professional success, late night carousing, and reliance on past achievement were not satisfying his calling, Steve reached out to a new beginning at Deerfield High School. Would his formula succeed for a program and a community that were unfamiliar with the kind of excellence Steve hoped to revive? As he matured as a teacher, coach, and man at Deerfield, he was inspired to share his knowledge almost as if he knew his time to share was limited. He hosted a coaching class at DHS. We left his course reeling with imagination and armed with dozens of strategies and concepts. He encouraged his students (coaches) to celebrate the goodness in people, while reminding us how important our roles were to the players' lives we were influencing.

Steve wryly taught us a fool-proof underneath the basket inbound play designed for, as Steve called him, his "Osco Guy." Steve implored us to develop strategies, plays, and specials that would specifically highlight the value of our less talented role players. His Osco Guy needed to work late nights and weekends at the local drugstore to help his family pay bills and tuition. Steve respected the unsung guys trying to stay afloat in the world of high school. Rather than exclude or humiliate these kids for not committing fully to basketball, Steve sought opportunities to help the Osco Drugstore Guys succeed. He taught us a remarkably simple, yet remarkably effective cross screen at the blocks where Osco screens away for MVP. The defenders inevitably collapse on the MVP leaving Osco all alone on the weak-side block for a lay-in. Steve employed a treasury of these types of misdirection plays, providing opportunities for less privileged players by deploying his MVP's as decoys. Not only were they tactically successful, but they built trust, confidence, and democracy in the team concept. Everyone had value in Steve's world.

The concept of TEAM defined and dictated the vision by which Steve Pappas lived. He and his wife Cathie shared a car with the license plate TEAMMATES. His voice mail greeting closed with "and remember, TEAM FIRST!" Steve committed his entire life both on and off the court facilitating team work, encouraging collaborative relationships, and sharing rich moments of laughter and triumph with all of us fortunate to know him. In large group presentations and conversations, he would begin his remarks by summarizing and bolstering the ideas of previous speakers. "Dennis and Karl make strong points about process; we should follow their lead." Then, Steve would enhance the ideas with his own keen insights. By affirming others and connecting his agenda to theirs, he seamlessly moved initiatives, built consensus, and advanced collaboration. Similarly, when teaching or presenting, Steve respected the process of epiphany and allowed his students and participants the freedom to generate their own thinking, often leading to conclusions more personally derived, hence more profound, than those Steve had intended. Steve frequently relinquished control to his students, a practice that only exceptional leaders understand.

Steve Pappas was unafraid. Prior to major events, his habits were unaltered. He valued pre-game conversation with his adversaries to a point where some opposing coaches suspected Steve of playing mind games. Always grounded, his teams relied on his unflappable nature and performed consistently themselves. Eventually, opposing coaches understood Steve's affable demeanor and grew to appreciate the fellowship that he naturally promoted with his brothers in coaching.

When angry parents assaulted Steve with criticism and disappointment in his decision making, rather than respond defensively, he welcomed them in, listened intently, and collaborated with them to improve the situation. More times than not, those critical parents became strong allies, once they understood the innate kindness and educational wisdom of Steve Pappas. He admitted in retrospect, that many of those types of challenges inspired his best work.

Steve Pappas was committed to an all-inclusive learning community as reflected in Proverbs 27:17, "As iron sharpens iron, men sharpen men." Cathie provided further insight into this man.

He was so good about letting you know what he borrowed from somebody else. One of the best things he did for our English department was to help people understand that we can give credit to other people for the good things. We don't have to be the owner of all ideas. It's okay to say, 'you know what, because of your input, I solved this or I absorbed that or whatever.' But Steve was constantly having conversations like that and he was so good.

He could give away stuff. He just gave it all away. I remember saying to him one time regarding basketball. You know the calls are coming into the office like nuts. I'm picking up the phone: Hey, is Steve there? No. Will you tell him that I…I need this. And so one time I said, "Steve don't you play those guys?"

"Yeah."

"Well, you're giving them all your stuff."

"Well, it's a part of the fraternity. It's like how we do it. It's okay." And that was it. And that's how he lived out being a teacher.

It was a real learning lesson for me. He gave away…and that was the other thing. He didn't care if it was perfect or not perfect, you just need this? Okay. He didn't care if you were coming back. He couldn't care less. If this helps you, then go for it. I was always amazed by that, especially at Deerfield. It's not that kind of culture. I mean they want you to be collaborative but everything is like judged. And I knew on occasion it might not be good for him. But he was always giving stuff away. Always, always, always. He took great pleasure in doing that. Those things you guys did a couple of times. He so liked that idea where you would get together and have think tanks [coaches roundtables]. (Cathie Pappas)

Steve asked me from time to time to address his teams at Deerfield High School. I relished these opportunities. His players welcomed me in to their special fraternity. Unlike most high school kids, these young men confidently smiled and shook my hand, asked of my needs, and thanked me for joining them. They listened intently to what I presented and then genuinely asked questions to clarify their understanding. My first visit, I callously believed that Steve commanded them to be on their best behavior, but after receiving this respect time and time again, I realized that this respectful learning community that Steve created must have been a joy to work with each day.

Steve engineered that joyful community. To this day, those players make a point to check up on me and acknowledge me when we cross paths. They do this because they don't know any other way. Steve taught them that the basketball community deserves their respect and the basketball community returned that respect to the players of Gordon Tech and Deerfield High Schools.

The File Cabinets of Coach Pappas

Steve's widow, Cathie Pappas, selected files, charts, notes, quotes, posters, and other telling evidence of the brilliance of Steve Pappas. The items are randomly organized. Steve was highly organized, but highly *randomly* organized. Any effort to micromanage his files would have interfered with the flow of energy with which he relied. Coach flourished in random situations which kept him fresh, learning, and alive.

Duke University's Coach Krzyzewski once remarked at a clinic that over preparation can be as damaging as under preparation. He used as an example his belief that a final practice plan must not be prepared until that morning of practice. His point: as the team evolves, important factors change that must be acknowledged each day, each hour. A practice plan devised days, weeks, or months in advance loses relevance with each passing hour. Steve would have echoed Coach K's position. Ironically, Steve's arsenal of teaching materials filled dozens of filing cabinets. Included in the next few pages are brief summaries of these materials.

Mr. Pappas' Magic List

Explorer John Goddard wrote an article about things he wanted to do in his lifetime. The yellowed pages and ancient font suggested that the article was written pre-1980, long before Lou Holtz's list, or Hollywood's movie *The Bucket List*. Steve used this list to teach students and players about goal setting.

Practice Plans

Steve archived his practice plans over the years. Plans from his early days at Gordon were reviewed prior to formulating new plans each season. A complete agenda for each of his assistants as well as a master "To-Do List" for Steve himself were reviewed and updated annually. His attention to detail was incredible, especially in his efforts to create a program calendar and scope and sequence chronicling the development of players' skill sets from freshman through varsity. Every member of his program had access to a well-defined roadmap to success. Steve left no stones unturned.

Quotes, Ideas, and Inspiration

As I poured over hundreds of Steve's documents, it became clear that Steve's focus had little to do with X's and O's, strategies, and statistics. Steve built strong men. He endeavored to surround himself with powerful, clear thinking, and loving men. His hope was to prepare these men to wield their power on the world to improve the lives they would soon encounter.

Handwritten Notes, Quotes, and Scrawls

The following constitute a small sampling of the inspirational guideposts that shaped the life of Steve Pappas.

> "Truth telling is more important than peacekeeping.
> Don't get mired in comfort."

"I lay down my life for the sheep."
~John 10:10–15

"I don't care where you are—but are you going somewhere?"

"Blame nobody, expect nothing, do something."

"We cannot become what we need to be by remaining what we are."

"If you hurry through life without giving God time, this world will seem like
a hospital, a place to get sick and die. If you go through life with God, this
world will seem like an inn, a place to stay while you're passing through."

"God gave us our memories so that we might have roses in December."
~Sir James Barrie

"That is us. That is not us."

"We can win this one through our brotherhood."

"Unfinished business."

"I look around and I see love…and the love keeps coming.
With a humble heart I want to tell *you* that I am eternally grateful.
God bless you. Teammates always."

Influences

Steve developed his philosophy by paying attention. He possessed the knack for
gleaning excellence from others. He crossed paths with exceptional coaches,
among them: Bob Ociepka, Chicago Bulls; Phil Jackson, Los Angeles Lakers;
Lute Olsen, University of Arizona; Don Myer, David Lipscomb University;
Bear Bryant, University of Alabama; and countless others.

Steve embraced ideas and learned from his peers, among them: Gene Pingatore, Saint Joseph; Mike Kolze, Highland Park High School; Jim Tracy, Reavis High School; Dennis Zelasko, Notre Dame High School; Will Rey, Northridge Prep; Dave Scott, Maine South High School, and Jerry Leggett, Quincy High School.

He read voraciously and selected passages from literature that would help clarify ideas for his students and players. Steve was an ardent fan of film, often choosing clips to hammer home points of importance. He listened carefully for lyrics in songs and concepts in advertising. Steve constantly quoted Emerson, Lincoln, Gandhi, Lombardi, Parcells, Wooden, and others. The following are quotes which repeatedly surfaced on his practice plans, bulletin board materials, presentations, and lectures.

"I am a part of all that I have met."
~Tennyson

"God can do anything, you know, far more than you could ever imagine or guess or request in your wildest dreams."
~Ephesians 3:20

The Quaker Newsletter

John Wooden's Pyramid of Success

"The enemy is nameless and faceless."
~Leonidas, Spartan warrior

Verbs: English Teaching Humor

Imagine being a stringer for the prep page of the local newspaper, covering thousands of contests each year that require verbiage of a repetitive nature. Steve loved the verbs! He would rate a victory by the verb the prep writer chose. "Upended," "breezed," "fended off," "laughed," "beat," "upset," and "pounded" are typical selections. "Pummeled" was a verb that found a prominent place in the legend of Steve Pappas.

Most Told Steve Pappas Story

For years, Catholic League lower-level teams ventured to 79th and Sangamon to receive a mental, physical, and spiritual pummeling (to use one of Coach Pappas' favorite verbs) at the hands of the Leo Lions in their tiny bandbox of a gym. These weren't 10 or 20 point embarrassments. These were shellackings punctuated by broken noses, lost teeth, and multiple contusions. Coaches around the league were convinced that Leo's strategy was to humiliate teams at the lower levels, forever scarring them and reducing them to vulnerable varsity squads in the future. Leo High School enjoyed a decade of dominance during the 1980s. Finally, one evening at Gordon Tech High School, the tide began to turn. Late in the third quarter, Gordon's Rams led by all-stater Tom Kleinschmidt were pummeling the Lions of Leo. Up by 25 points, Coach Pappas elected to leave his starters in and their suffocating press on as the quarter neared its end. Catholic league legend and Leo High School coach, Jack Fitzgerald, was upset and puzzled by Steve's choice to run up the score. Coach Pappas was known for integrity, sportsmanship, and fairness. Fitz walked past the scorer's table and called to Steve, "Hey Steve, what the fuck?" Steve, who was standing and orchestrating the blow out with particular zeal, turned to Fitz and charged him with a crazed grin as Rams are known to do and replied, "What the fuck? What the fuck Fitz? For decades you have pummeled us beyond humiliation! What the fuck?" At that moment, Kleinschmidt pulled up from 30 feet and drained a 3-pointer. Steve lifted both hands over his head signaling the three and grinned from ear to ear. "That a boy Tommy! Let's walk the dog!" Jack Fitzgerald sulked back to his bench and sat down while Steve uncharacteristically high-fived his players and staff the rest of the game, sending the once mighty Lions to an embarrassing submission.

No one could tell that story better than Steve and he was coerced into telling that story dozens of times whenever a contingent of Catholic leaguers shared stories and brew. Steve would light up when telling the Leo story: (a) because it grew in its popularity at every telling and provoked all of Steve's talents as a performing artist; (b) the story was typically shared with "veteran" coaches who, as Steve would say, "did their term in Nam" (Steve's description of coaching in the volatile Catholic League). Most importantly, the story was the classic underdog finally overcoming the legendary nemesis. Steve fought for underdogs and was a passionate soldier for social justice.

Snapshots

Karl Costello, former roommate, colleague, and friend recalled the spiritual force that guided Steve Pappas—balance:

> My wife and I were out in Arizona last year for our anniversary; I didn't bring my golf clubs because we went up to Sedona. Steve recommended for years that I visit this sacred place that he encountered during his college years at Grand Canyon College. I had never been to Sedona. As soon as I got up there and was surrounded by these monuments and these rocks and we pulled off on this one trail. You know, this is Steve. This is Steve. Now I understand even more. Then I connected with all those times when we were living together; like he would go out for runs sometimes at 10 o'clock at night. The guy was a physical specimen. He didn't go out for a run for physical… but the real reason he would go out for a run, I guess it is metaphysical because he needed to become…one with the universe. Clear his mind. Here's a typical evening. We actually made a tape of all-time great scenes from movies. So we're sitting there watching this scene from *The Sons of Katie Elder* where John Wayne bashes George Kennedy in the face with a bat, okay, or Clint Eastwood, you know, meeting with Ten Bears: "[Spit] I reckon so." You know: "Will there be blood or will there be life? There will be life." A cut from *Blues Brothers*. We just fell over with laughter, you know, scene after scene after scene, and then it would be like 10:30 at night after a

long day of teaching, coaching, and a few beers. I was cashed. Steve would stand up and say, "I'm going for a run." He needed balance. (Karl Costello)

Wake Up Call

Karl Costello recalled one of many instances when Steve demonstrated remarkable kindness:

> One time we went to the Olive Branch, Eddy's bar [Steve called his dad Eddy] at Peterson and California to watch Monday Night Football. We'd go there, have a hamburger on black bread, and watch the game. We closed the joint at 3 a.m. Later that Tuesday morning, he left me at our apartment to sleep in, went to school, and took care of my first class. Then he came back and got me up to go. When I woke, I freaked thinking I would be fired for missing my first period assignment. Steve calmly assured me that he had it covered. He was always doing stuff like that. There is no better man. I haven't seen him… there is no one. (Karl Costello)

Inclusion

Dan Sakan, former player and volunteer coach, shared a story about Pappas generosity and his sense of community:

> When I coached with him in the last year that he coached, I was working downtown and I hadn't really been doing anything with basketball or baseball and I wanted to get involved again, so I went to Steve and asked him if I could help out and he said, "Well, you need to get your certification and come in whenever you want." So I took my classes so I could be certified and got to at least be there on game days to help on the bench. During the regional IHSA tournament, we won our first round game as an 8th seed, which meant that we were going to go on the road to Libertyville, the number one seed that year. The Libertyville

gym was insane. Just insane. We were going nuts with time-out situations and we were winning for most of the second half and the crowd was going insane. When the final buzzer rang, it was a moment that surpassed any I had during my playing days. It was just incredible. And then we were cutting down the nets because we won the Regionals. Everyone had gone up to get their turn and there was only one more cut to be made and it's going to be Steve's cut. He invited me up the ladder to make the cut with him. I wasn't planning on going up there. I showed up once a week on game days. What did I do?

So we climbed the ladder together and held the net together and it was a moment I'll never forget. He wanted to share success with everyone else. I mean it was just very touching for everyone and he never forgot. He reminds me of that all the time. He really appreciated that. (Dan Sakan)

The Sunshine of Steve Pappas

Dennis Zelasko, friend and former colleague, described a time during the Gordon Tech years that captures the Pappas Perspective. In the early eighties, long before his exceptional career as an NBA coach, Head Coach Bob Ociepka, master motivator and program builder, assembled an all- star coaching staff. Please read Coach Zelasko's humorous story with an appreciation for the Pappas values: clear head, calm, unafraid, and free. Coach Pappas often assessed situations very differently than his peers:

While at Gordon Tech, Bob Ociepka, who is fanatically organized, got a playbook that we updated the beginning of every season and the playbook is this black, three-ring binder that's probably about 500 pages. Every year, he's got like 75 new pages; take out section B, you know, put this back in. And it's a pretty intense thing, but it just so happens that we both had children, our first children born. He had Katie [who] was born that summer and our oldest son Matt was born that summer and Bob loosened up just slightly from maybe Genghis Khan to you know Attila the Hun. So he decided he's going to have a barbecue at his house and he was going to bring the book and we're going to have a short meeting and then we're going to have the families there for a barbecue. So we go; we replace the pages we need to replace; we have a barbecue. And then it's time to go home and, of course, our first baby, you know, you got the diaper bag and the carry baby, the car seat and you've got a million things. So I've got the baby and the car seat and I got the diaper bag and I hand the book to Mary. So we go out to the car. I put the baby in the back seat, strap him in. And then Mary takes the book. She had other things in her hands. She puts the book on the top of the car, okay, and she leaves it there. We both get in the car; we look at each other, and say, "Do we have everything?" Yes. Okay. So we...Now the book is so heavy, that it stays on the car until we're turning on Harlem and Higgins onto the expressway to go home. You know, it's gone like five blocks and it's still up there, but it falls off as we're turning onto the expressway on Harlem Avenue. So we get home...

We get home and we're putting everything away and I go, "Hey, Mary, where's the book?" She says, "Well, you have the book." I said, "Well, no, you have the book. I gave it to you." She says, "Oh, I don't remember that." We look all over. She says, "I must have left it in Bob's living room." So now, again, if you knew Bob and you knew the time, okay, it's like I now have to make a call to his house and say to him that I left the 500-pound, you know, 500-page book in his living room which was supposed to be handcuffed to your wrist. You weren't supposed to ever walk around without this top secret book which detailed all of our schemes, you know. This is a very painful phone call. So I call him and he's telling me that the book is not at his house and I'm thinking that, you know, this is punishment for forgetting it; like he's not going to tell me and make me worry that I don't know where the book is. So we look again; we scour the house, and we look through everything and can't find it. I've got to call him back a second time. Okay? And so now he's hot and he's telling me: "I don't have your god dang book, you know." So we come up with the thought that well maybe we lost it; we left it on the roof of the car. Mary kind of remembers that she did it. So now Bob retraces our steps to the expressway and he gets to Harlem and Higgins and the book is in the middle of the street in a million pieces. Okay? And he's running down Harlem Avenue, picking up pages and trying to collect everything. So I call back a third time to the house and Ann answers the phone and I say, "Ann, let me talk to Bob." And she says, "No, you do not want to talk to Bob." I go, "No, no, Ann, I have to talk to Bob. I've got to find out what he did." She goes, "No trust me Denny; you do not want to talk to Bob." Okay? So it ends up that he had stuffed like the 500 pages in a brown Jewel bag and I had to meet him the next morning at like 6:30 in the morning at school.

Gordon had these like long hallways and I was at one end, he was at the other end walking towards me, and it was just like Gary Cooper in *High Noon*, you know. And he finally gets to me and he shoves the book into my chest and he goes, "Here's your fucking book." The funny part about all of this is that when I realized that I lost my book, I called Karl Costello, another assistant, immediately. I told him the whole story and I said…"Karl, what am I going to do? What do I do?" And there's this pause on the phone and then he comes back and goes: "Well, there's only one thing you can do. Resign. Quit. You gotta quit. There's nothing else you can do. You've lost the book. It's like the Bible, you know? You've gotta quit." So I go, "Hey Karl, thank you very much." You know, I hang up. It's not the advice I'm looking for. So now I immediately turn around and I call Steve, and explained the whole story to Steve, lost the book, and again there's a pause on the end of the phone, but Steve comes up with a little different twist on the whole scenario, a little bit different than Karl...

"Z, this is absolutely the best thing that ever happened to Bob Ociepka. He is wound way too tight and this is going to force him to loosen up and calm down and ultimately he's only going to have to laugh about it now." He goes: "It's the best thing that ever happened to our program." You know about the Pappas sunshine; that was it in a nutshell right there. One guy is telling me I should quit, you know, like it's the end of the world and Steve now thinks it's the best thing that's ever happened to our program. Well, after I got my book shoved in my chest from Bob, I realized you couldn't operate and coach unless you had the Bible. You know, it was like every situation was prescribed as to what you would do, you know, if you were down five and shooting a one and one with 42 seconds left, it's in the book. You would find the situations. So I ended up asking Karl to borrow his book so I could Xerox it but he refused to give it to me. It couldn't be let out of his sight. Steve says...absolutely. And this is like 1983 or '82, something like that. Xerox is like 3 cents a copy, you know, and I took the book to like Kinkos or whatever it was and it ended up costing me $78.00 to get that book replaced, you know. We gave Steve back his book and somewhere along the line, Bob didn't talk to me much for a good part of that year and maybe Mary for about five months and then somewhere

at the end of season, we ended up in a bar together and Steve
suggested that Mary should buy Bob a drink. Bob smiled and it
was over. God, I miss Steve. (Dennis Zelasko)

Steve's Affable Essence: When You Get Lemons

Dave Scott, basketball coach at Maine South remembered a night that displayed
the upbeat, always positive and accessible Coach Pappas:

Steve came to scout us at Maine South. We had a group of kids
that had these shirts that said: The Red Scare. As soon as Steve
walked in the gym, I think we played him [Deerfield] the next
week, and all these kids recognized him and started jeering
you know: Deerfield's Next! Most coaches would have ignored
the taunt, but Steve sat down right in front of them all and
was shaking hands with them all and said, "We'll be here next
week, Friday at 7:30" and stuff like that. He just had a ball with
them and when he saw me after the game he said, "I had fun
with the Red Scare guys." (Dave Scott)

Franklin Drobb provided his perspective as one of Steve's former students.
I include this recollection, not only for Frank's eloquence, but for Steve's impact
on this future educator. Simple respect, kindness, and affirmation mixed with
a common affinity for literature created a bond that will pay dividends for
hundreds of Frank's students:

I never viewed Steve Pappas as a coach because he never was
one for me in terms of a basketball coach. He and I shared a
relationship as two individuals who loved reading, loved the
idea of Homer's *Odyssey,* loved the idea of *Hamlet,* loved the
idea of McMurphy and Nurse Ratchet, but also loved the idea of
the Chief observing all of this and he's the one who broke free.

So the one time I did go to a basketball game and it was like
his 100th win and I had to be there. He was about to win this

big event. And we're in a big stadium, a lot of teenagers, a lot of hoopla, a lot of things going on and I was just at the top and the back, just observing Coach Pappas be coach. He raised his voice, not in terms yelling, but he's raising it to project. I was like he's never done that before. So it got pretty interesting and I enjoyed it, but the thing that touched me about that experience was Monday morning we came back to school and people were congratulating him on a job well done and he was like, "Yeah, and I saw you were there too Frank." He recognized me and that he also recognized that that was the only game I ever came to see him at. He was touched by that when he saw me there and that was just a really great moment.

What I also really enjoyed about Steve [are] the simple things that aren't talked about, like being in a hallway and seeing your students twice in five minutes when you pass each other by. Ninety-nine percent of people get awkward. They either look down, look at their watch, pretend like there is something going on all of sudden when you just saw somebody and said hi. Mr. Pappas always had a way of just being very genuine and authentic like: "Hey, are you following me?" So he always made those moments that would be perceived as awkward, casual, and I loved the fact that, as an educator, he never raised his voice; that actually when students became louder, he became quieter. That was one of the most powerful things that I've learned as an educator that has always passed on, the smile on his face. Looking back years now, he knew what was up—everything. He knew what was up, but he wouldn't make people feel bad about it; he didn't make students feel bad about it. He would accept them for what they were and let them work with what they had in front of them. So he wouldn't ever make me feel bad about getting a C, but he knew that I could get an A, and so I worked for the As, in his class only. So now here I am going to create a transformation in education in the classroom, all a result of a man who inspired me to go into education because he was calm. (Franklin Drobb)

Stargazer

The words of Mrs. Cathie Pappas affirmed the spiritual and metaphysical connection from which Coach Pappas drew in making sense of the world:

Every evening, I don't care if we had a game, or what was going on, or whatever time he came in, whether we lived in Deerfield or when we lived here in Libertyville, he would make me stand outside and look up to the sky. And he would tell me what he was seeing and then say, "Well, what do you see?" Well, I wasn't seeing as much as he was seeing, but I would have a little conversation. He knew the stars and the planets and he would talk about it. It was like hearing another story right before the day ends. (Cathie Pappas)

CHAPTER SEVEN

———————————————•———————————————

REFLECTIONS

American education has endured decades of scrutiny. Despite significant advances in test scores, curriculum design, teacher preparation, professional development, technological evolution, and a world that processes information at unprecedented speed, schools will continue to be held responsible for the health, safety, and overall success of American children. Our once proud and fiercely independent nation built upon the strength of family life expects miracles from our schools. Fortunately, educators like Rick Malnati, Steve Pappas, and Gene Pingatore met and surpassed this challenge every day. Next to socioeconomics, the classroom teacher is the most influential factor in the formula for a student's successful educational experience.

Findings

Beyond the entertainment value evoked from Gene Pingatore's family feasts, Steve Pappas' erudite references to flavor his stories of unparalleled irony, and Rick Malnati's vitriolic bursts of confrontation, the conversations included in this collection affirm that miracles are being performed by teachers and coaches every day. All three subjects of this study employed humor, tenacity, pride, and humility while building lifelong relationships that create stimulating learning experiences. These men of Chicago truly understood the concept of work and the benefits derived from honest labor and unyielding commitment toward incremental improvement. They preached it, lived it, and celebrated the joy of hard work. I admit I failed to unearth the gold mentioned earlier in this study. In fact, the term "gold" was dismissed quickly by each of the subjects. In one way or another, each declared that they had no secrets.

If they had no secrets, why did they lap the field so convincingly? The answer for all three may be as simple as the lottery slogan, "you can't win if you don't play." These men relished the purity of life, sought mountains to climb, respected pain and loss for its groundedness, and most commonly, squeezed the time they have on this earth to make a difference. None of them complained that life was unfair, work was too hard, or the demands placed upon them too great; yet, they each continued to give and give to the betterment of mankind. They didn't cut corners.

These men shared many commonalities. In their youth, all three were products of recently immigrated families, their fathers were rarely present at home, and their commitment to their mothers' well-being was extraordinary. Playgrounds, parks, and neighborhoods were their refuge. All were talented athletes, organizers, and initiators. Working class roots taught lessons about value, time, commitment, and a keen appreciation for simple things. Pain, defeat, and disappointment visited each of them as young children. They enjoyed being alone, but recognized valuable friendships which they sustained throughout their lives.

As educators, they willingly accepted the grueling time and energy commitments that defined their incredible power as change agents. They addressed challenges head on, truthfully, compassionately, and responsibly, regardless of backlash or political disfavor. A strong sense of foundational values provided them clarity as they made difficult decisions. They laughed boisterously and frequently, most often at themselves. Their willingness to reach way beyond what was expected of them in support of their students combined with highly developed emotional intelligence built unshakable trust. Critical self-reflection haunted each of them, yet served as the spark for their next mission and they were always on a mission.

They were master story tellers. They knew how to engage a listener, employing expression, tone, rhythm, body language, humor, irony, and passion. Their stories were most often parables with the intention of imprinting valuable lessons in students' minds. Socially comfortable and exceedingly charismatic, these were men of substance and students and colleagues were drawn to their foundational strength.

The teaching field is rife with institutional instructors who learned their craft in textbooks and seminars. Malnati, Pingatore, and Pappas escaped that mold and shared their distinctly refreshing ideology. A courageous toughness was present and was enhanced each time they got knocked down. Risk takers and educators of principle get knocked down. These gritty warriors endured countless knock downs and earned countless recoveries. Their hopeful and resilient nature was bolstered by their love for the arena and their belief in the goodness of people.

They knew where they were going and were clear in their presentation of that vision. Simple, pragmatic, collaborative, and supportive are qualities that guide students naturally toward the vision. It helped that they were uncommonly likable. Maya Angelou's quote captured their essence, "People may forget what you said and did, but will never forget how you made them feel."

The purpose of this study was to examine the strategies, characteristics, habits, patterns, and philosophies of leaders in education. Exceptional teaching and exceptional learning environs are the only responses schools can provide to the unreasonable demands that American society places upon them. The three Coaches of Chicago very clearly distinguished themselves as exceptional.

Revisiting the Question

What can we learn from the stories of these extraordinary coaches that will help us to become more insightful teachers and confident leaders?

During the course of this study, Malnati, Pappas, and Pingatore provided generous and more importantly, thoughtful perspectives on educating student athletes. These candid conversations led to many valuable frameworks of pedagogy. Four recurring themes linked to teaching, learning, and leadership emerged from the interviews that very accurately define the success of these self-actualized educators: Work Ethic, Keen Observation and Listening Skills, Resilience, and Integrity.

Theme One: Work Ethic

At the foundation of this study's participants' many successes, is their relentless commitment to the highest quality of work. The words of Chicago writer and icon Studs Terkel help to define the approach to work that these men employed each and every day as educators.

> It is about a search for daily meaning as well as daily bread, for recognition as well as for cash, for astonishment rather than torpor, for a sort of life rather than a Monday through Friday sort of dying. Perhaps immortality too is part of the quest.

These coaches were driven by an obligation to excellence and an insatiable curiosity about the limits of human spirit and human achievement. When solving problems, time becomes just a nuisance, fatigue a mere distraction, and the flow created inspires new ideas and joyful urgency

Malnati learned about the nature of work in the pizza kitchens while his family grew the business; Pingatore lived through the post-Depression era and witnessed firsthand the desperation of finding work and finding food; Pappas rarely saw his parents who worked incredibly long work days. These men lived more by P.T. Barnum's "the harder I work, the luckier I get," than by Woody Allen's "eighty percent of life is showing up." Malnati admitted that fear of failure and embarrassment motivates him to outwork, out hustle, and out prepare his opponents, but he also described the state of euphoria experienced during moments of well-prepared triumph. He pushed players to capacity, hoping they will build self-confidence and understand the role work ethic plays in their quest for power. Pingatore leaned on the lessons his mother provided him about completion of work, organization of details, and consistent refinement. He demanded a family type loyalty to the quality of work and his Chargers met that challenge for over 50 years. Pappas marched to the beat of a different drummer. Like Odysseus, Steve viewed work as an odyssey, an adventure to travel through the volatile peaks and lulls of a season. Without hard work, the *rarified air* of March Madness cannot be savored.

These coaches endeavored to build cathedrals. Coaching in competitive Chicago did not satisfy their yearning for creating unchartered journeys toward perfection. They chose to raise expectations and share a life with their players that demanded and celebrated what the Greeks referred to as *Arête*, exceptional excellence. The level of devotion necessary to achieve Arête inspires innovation around the world and is stunningly apparent in the work ethic of these gentlemen. Thriving schools are led by people who immerse themselves completely and authentically, people willing to selflessly commit to a level similar to that of the subjects of this study. University of Wisconsin's Bo Ryan was fond of the definitions of "involvement" and "commitment" taught to him by local farmers. When you sit down and enjoy a country breakfast, the chicken that provided the eggs was "involved" while the pig that provided the bacon was "committed." Malnati, Pappas, and Pingatore would certainly garner respect from Wisconsin farmers.

Roland Barth asserted that schools can only grow if the principal is willing and able to grow. A commitment to lifelong learning is shared among Malnati, Pingatore, and Pappas. Twenty-five years ago, young coaches quizzically wondered why Ping, an accomplished and decorated coach atop his profession, attended coaching clinics and conferences. Well, he continued to turn every stone in his quest for improved understanding by reading the latest books, scouring the Web, hosting conversations, seeking input, establishing new relationships, and attending any clinic that may shed light on this great game. I marvel at Rick Malnati's zealous approach to learning the nuances of college basketball as he traveled his recent path at Loyola University. Steve Pappas was voracious in his love for new ideas. Unlike many coaches, he looked to history, sociology, philosophy, and the arts for his inspiration. His teams exhibited incomparable poise and celebration for each competitive moment, no doubt attributable to the creative blending of dissonant ideas filtered through the genius of Pappas. Barth would understand why Malnati, Pingatore, and Pappas and their learning communities have enjoyed such remarkable growth. Their relentless pursuit of deeper understanding is reflective of their approach to work.

Finally, the three subjects of this study all understood that service and sacrifice are cornerstones to the strength of a team. By constantly modeling service to others, their students grew to respect the power and energy created through service. Coach Pappas often shared the following passage with his teams and the many coaches whom he mentored:

> I will tell his majesty what a king is. A king does not abide within his tent while his men die and bleed upon the field. A king does not dine while his men go hungry; nor sleep when they stand watch upon the wall. A king does not command his men's loyalty through fear nor purchase it with gold; he earns their love by the sweat of his own back and the pains he endures for their sake. That which comprises the harshest burden, a king lifts first and sets down last. A king does not require service of those he heads but provides it to them. He serves them, not they him. (Pressfield)

I have witnessed dozens of young coaches hungry to climb into the spotlight only to meet with unceremonious departures from the profession of teaching and coaching. To sustain a career in leadership requires an uncompromised commitment to work. A job without problems is not a job. Good work is achieved at a price and that price is not short lived bursts of adrenalin, but a steady, passionate, and unyielding approach to excellence. Friday nights in jam packed arenas orchestrating a team to victory is a sliver of the genuine coach experience. Most coaches, many great coaches, toil in obscurity, work long hours that all but destroy personal and family life, never knowing the pomp and glory of regional and sectional championships. Malnati, Pingatore, and Pappas savored the work, savored those few glorious moments a fortunate career may render. More importantly, they respected the work and recognized that anything shy of their level best was unacceptable. Most importantly, they found ways to include their loved ones in the journey. Frankly, their respect for work is daunting and intimidating. All three exhorted, "there are no short cuts."

Theme Two: Keen Observation and Listening Skills

Every study of educational leadership includes the necessity for open and collaborative communication. The ability to convey a vision and its components is an essential quality for leaders, but a striking similarity among the subjects of this study distinguishes and prioritizes the definition of communication to observing and listening. Successful leaders speak carefully only after extensive periods of observation and listening. Whether it is Ping's intuitive evaluation of athletic prowess, Malnati's analysis of his team's demeanor in a huddle, or Pappas' patient silence that allowed players to resolve conflict among themselves, it is clear that effective leaders observe; effective leaders listen.

From observing and listening, the effective leader is informed as he creates his vision and implements his plans. The Coaches of Chicago emphasized the value of learning about one's ever-changing organization and the daily, subtle movement that left unacknowledged could emerge as an unintended sea change.

Each subject involved in this study demonstrated consistent respect for observation and listening, particularly during the extremes of invincibility and vulnerability. Pappas' mantra, "the enemy is nameless and faceless" reminded players to focus on the task as opposed to the personal and particular details of an encounter. Wooden respected passionate yet emotionless play. Machine-like precision and stoic demeanor characterized his UCLA Bruins during their nine year run of consecutive national championships. The Trevians relied on Malnati's consistently intense approach toward perfection, regardless of wins, losses, championships, or failures. Consistent precision and unshakable stoicism are qualities demonstrated by the teams coached by this study's subjects. They developed healthy and open "performance systems" (Longenecker & Pinkel), encouraging a "participatory universe" (Wheatley), paying particular attention to their "athletes' perceptions" (Carron & Bennett). At the outset of this study, I anticipated that these very different coaches would embody some of the elements discovered in my research of the literature; yet, I have learned that in their own ways, each of these coaches mastered most of the findings connected to communication and its critical relationship to team building.

NBA's Phil Jackson built his career on finding a structure that empowers *everybody*. Like Lombardi and Krzyzewski, he was blessed with an extraordinary "intrapersonal awareness" (Donaldson) that sensed high cognitive anxiety (Kenow & Williams). The work of Malnati, Pingatore, and Pappas reflected the importance of this trait, and respected that intrapersonal awareness as high school coaches bled beyond the locker room and into relationships with assistant coaches, parents, administration, feeder programs, media, and other colleagues. All of these constituents were capable of disturbing the momentum of the program if cognitively anxious. "The problems of the system are the problems of the smallest unit." (Elmore) Attention to detail is one of the most overused phrases in coaching, but when it involves observing and listening, attention to detail is paramount and intrapersonal awareness in this regard served Malnati, Pingatore, and Pappas well.

The best learning systems inspire students to acquire their own education as opposed to passively receiving learning from a teacher-centered environment. Player collaboration and player ownership are hallmarks of championship caliber teams. Careful observation followed by patient listening invites collaboration and ownership which rescues the smart coach from pulling his team up the mountain. Most basketball players are asked by most basketball coaches to comply with the system and surrender their own innate creativity. These coaches are suffocating their teams. Through observing and listening, the subjects of this study invited players to share their creativity and listened to all stakeholders throughout the running conversation that shaped their program's distinguished journey. Many talented players possess dominant personalities. If the coach is the dominant personality, there is little room for those exceptional players to lead and grow. Most coaches struggle with this dynamic, but this study's subjects respected the nature of relinquishing power to the players. The coach becomes vulnerable, but that openness invites players to own their fate.

"The objective in any team sport is to transform the group from a mere collection of talented individuals into a highly cohesive unit so that the whole is greater than the sum of its parts." (Dicicco) As a team evolves, the coach must not only observe and listen, but accurately analyze the behaviors of his team. Malnati, Pingatore, and Pappas consistently developed teams that became greater than the sum of their parts. In many instances, these coaches confronted behaviors detrimental to the health of the team. Coaches able to analyze behaviors and then respectfully confront detrimental behaviors in order for a team to grow are equipped with virtuoso interpersonal skills. (Goleman) Heider's definition of leadership captured the subjects' abilities to lead with water-like qualities—cleansing, fluid, and responsive. Keen observation and listening skills pave the way for educators to be effective responders.

Theme Three: Resilience

In 1982, during my first year of coaching, I attended a clinic that featured Lockport High School's Bob Basarich. He pointed his opening remarks at the many young coaches in attendance, asserting that everyone in the room will eventually be fired or asked to resign their coaching positions. The two hundred plus coaches chuckled at his remark, but Basarich proceeded to explain all the reasons that would contribute to our dismissals; these included politics, change in administration, the unpredictable nature of teen behavior, wins, losses, and others. Five years later, the innovative Bob Basarich was dismissed after a distinguished 20-year career. Since that clinic, I have witnessed the parade of coach dismissals. Job security is not one of our perks, which underscores the resilient abilities of Malnati, Pingatore, and Pappas.

The subjects of this study encountered failure, loss, humility, and public scrutiny, yet found ways to not only survive but thrive from the lessons learned and the toughness earned. Abolitionist newspaperman, Horace Greely wrote about President Lincoln:

> He was not a born king of men...but a child of the common people, who made himself a great persuader, therefore a leader, by dint of firm resolve, patient effort, and dogged perseverance. He slowly won his way to eminence and fame by doing the work that lay next to him—doing it with all his growing might—doing it as well as he could, and learning by his failure, when failure was encountered, how to do it

better…He was open to all impressions and influences, and gladly profited by the teachings of events and circumstances, no matter how adverse or unwelcome. There was probably no year of his life when he was not a wiser, cooler, and better man than he had been the year preceding." (Phillips)

Comparing basketball coaches to the great emancipator is not my intention, but Greeley's eloquent description of Lincoln's resilience, particularly his ability to stay the course during tragedy and controversy, can serve as a summary of the three subjects in my study. Their constant return to work, revising, tweaking, persevering, and confronting are all documented. Like Lincoln, they "gladly profited by the teachings" of adversity and improved incrementally through time. (Phillips) Reeves and Robinson both wrote about the value of learning to be a leader and its relationship to those career-long learners who steadily improved their acumen. Phil Jackson described coaching as messy and fraught with pain; yet, with a clear mind and open heart, coaches like this study's subjects build structures, set conditions, guide processes to the point where they trust their work. Malnati, Pingatore, and Pappas each possessed an internal confidence that appeared unshakable.

Paul Tough asked, "How do our experiences in childhood make us the adults we become?" Taking this question further and applying it to this study, how valuable are resilience and character strength in the development of an educator? Malnati, Pingatore, and Pappas experienced countless situations of immense gravity requiring timely and level-headed decision making. The frequent practices of evaluation, action, reflection, and revision improved these leaders. They endured in a cut-throat career by evolving through constant self-improvement. Selecting teams, assigning roles and playing time, encouraging the dominant scorers within the selected system of play while discouraging role players from launching unwelcomed field goal attempts, are all dangerously loaded decisions that undoubtedly will invite criticism and erode political capital. Coaches are routinely fired at the high school level for reasons ranging from winning percentage to likability, from political disfavor to philosophical disagreement. In a critical world of increasing accountability, young teachers shy away from coaching because of the nakedness of open public scrutiny. The growing reliance on numerical measures and standardization discourage educators from genuinely engaging students. (Zhao) In a quantitative world focused on content and the bottom line, the coach educators in this study thrived by respecting individual learning and valuing the immeasurability of the human spirit. Unfortunately, American education trends indicate that we would rather compete than create, and the freedom to create innovative excellence may be exchanged for a more systematized, teacher-proofed curriculum that would all but stifle the brilliance of this study's subjects and anyone else reaching for excellence, regardless of one's resilience. Fortunately, Malnati, Pingatore, Pappas and educators like them leave indelible impressions about the methodology necessary to inspire powerful learning.

Theme Four: Integrity

Malnati, Pappas, and Pingatore shared the trait of integrity with Wooden, Jackson, Riley, Lombardi, and Krzyzewski. All have pushed the envelope to the letter of the law. All have been tempted and refused to circumvent or manipulate the law. All have respected the universal ways of karma. The long careers of Malnati, Pingatore, and Pappas are testament that they conducted their business in a manner beyond reproach. Cheating may garner short term success for some coaches, but as we have seen through history, any hint of scandal erodes credibility and typically unravels a team and the coach leading that team. "The powerful influence of example should be a sacred trust for all of those who are in the position to help mold the character of young people in their formative years." (Wooden) Not only are coaches entrusted with the moral character development of their students, but one or two ethical errors will reveal to students a pattern not to be trusted. Lombardi cracked about the improbability of hoodwinking his players, which echoes the stories shared by and about the subjects of this study when they were faced with ethical dilemma.

Chelladurai and Saleh, throughout their study of athlete/coach compatibility, specifically mentioned athletes' preferences for integrity in the coach who leads them. Goleman spoke of the value of genuine relationship allowing for genuine feedback. The coach educators in this study were able to communicate genuinely with their players because every single decision they made enhanced their integrity. Coach John Gorleski of Highland Park High School channeled Emerson, "Your actions speak so loudly, I can barely hear your words."

Football Coach Gary Barnett spoke frequently about his role as coach and the privilege to serve his team and community. This study's subjects naturally served others. They selected the coaching vocation to provide proper guidance in all aspects of life, not just basketball. I respect the level of investment Malnati, Pingatore, and Pappas maintained in the lives of their former players. Weeks before Steve Pappas died, scores of his former players attended his induction into the IBCA Hall of Fame. They arrived armed with meaningful stories and memories of the days enjoyed with Coach Pappas. They gushingly shared these stories and competed for Steve's attention to report their latest achievements. Coach Pingatore enjoyed a similar rapport with his ex-Chargers. To his credit, they sent their children to Ping knowing that their progeny would experience the same life lessons they learned decades ago. As for Coach Malnati, it's not by accident that the Trevian-faithful loyally attend Fenwick HS contests miles from the North Shore.

Future Possibilities

This book examined wily veterans of exceptional talent who excelled in their craft for decades. The vast majority of coaches don't meet with this level of success. Why did Coaches Malnati, Pingatore, and Pappas navigate failure and right the ship while others struggle and often submerge? A careful examination of fledgling coaches, when compared to the three coaches in this study, may lead to important questions about innate ability, academic and leadership preparedness, work ethic, emotional intelligence, and the evolution of an educator during the course of one's career.

Malnati, Pingatore, and Pappas operated within supportive infrastructures. They worked in schools that valued athletic excellence and this was reflected in their staffing, facilities, feeder programs, community involvement, and financial investment. Professor Yong Zhao asserted that co and extra-curricular education is at the root of the innovation advantage Americans enjoy globally. As education funding declines, how will extra-curricular programming be sustained?

Many successful educators invest 40 hours of work per week, enjoy semester breaks, and two months summer vacation, while Malnati, Pingatore, and Pappas freely chose 80-hour work weeks, little if any down time, and a summer committed to basketball excellence. Coaches don't coach for the meager financial stipend, typically one tenth of their teacher salary. How can the same educational system have such disparity? A study of work/life balance may uncover solutions toward healthier lifestyles for coaches.

Many exceptional classroom teachers happen to coach an extra-curricular sport or activity. Are these coaches academic leaders in their subject areas? Are coaches perceived as lesser academicians because of pre-existing stereotypes about sports and jocks? Coaches are natural student engagers and utilize data-driven student achievement strategies. Are these coaches tapped by traditional instructors to learn about building strong relationships and collaborative learning communities? Has the data been mined to support the concept that strong extra-curricular programming is linked to academic performance? If such a relationship exists, will school districts be inspired to fund extra-curricular programs commensurately?

In a world of increasing data-driven accountability, is there still room for the simple joy of learning for the sake of learning? Will sports programming become a refuge for students interested in participation for the simple motivation of loving the game? Many students attend school primarily to maintain eligibility for participation in extracurricular activities. What can we learn as educators about this phenomenon to celebrate the values of teamwork, collaboration, problem solving, individuality, and creativity that many of our students have already discovered?

Personal Reflection

A day does not go by without a thought, concept, story, or inspiration that grabs me and requires me to reflect upon the work of the generous men in this study. Their stories provide tremendous guidance to me as a high school principal. Candidly, they inspire me to be a better human being. I have enjoyed the privilege of accessing these accounts and will be forever changed by what I have learned.

REFERENCES

Auerbach, A. (1985). *On and off the court*. New York, NY: Macmillan.

Barnett, G. (1996). *High hopes, taking the purple to Pasadena*. New York, NY: Warner Books.

Barth, R. (1985, March). The principalship. *Educational Leadership, 92*.

Bernard, H. R. (1988). *Research methods in cultural anthropology*. Newbury Park, CA: Sage Publications.

Bradley, B. (1977, October 31). You can't buy heart. *Sports Illustrated*, 104–109.

Brenner, M. E. (2006). Interviewing in educational research. In J. Green, G. Camilli & P. Elmore (Eds.), *Handbook of complementary methods in educational research*, (pp.357–370). Washington, DC: American Educational Research Association/ Erlbaum.

Brill, S. (2008). *Leading and learning*. Portland, ME: Stenhouse Publishing.

Carron, A. V., & Bennett, B. B. (1977). Compatibility in the coach-athlete dyad. *Research Quarterly, 48*, 671–679.

Chelladurai, P. (1978). *A contingency model of leadership in athletics*. Unpublished dissertation, University of Waterloo, Canada.

Chelladurai, P., & Saleh, S. D. (1980). Dimensions of leader behavior in sports: Development of a leadership scale. *Journal of Sport Psychologist, 6*, 344–357.

Clandinin, D. J., & Connelly, F. M. (2006). Narrative inquiry. In J. L. Green & G. Camilli, *Handbook of complementary methods in education research* (pp. 477-487). Mahwah, NJ. Lawrence Erlbaum Publishers.

Coles, R. (1989). *The call of stories: Teaching and the moral imagination*. Boston, MA: Houghton-Mifflin.

Collins, J. (2005). *Good to great and the social sectors*. Boulder, CO: Collins.

Creswell, J. W. (1998). *Qualitative inquiry and research design: Choosing among five traditions*. Thousand Oaks, CA: Sage Publications.

Cuban, L. (2004, April). Meeting challenges in urban schools. *Educational Leadership*, 64.

Cuban, L. (2011). Teacher, superintendent, scholar. In W. J. Urban (Ed.), *Leaders in the historical study of American education* (pp.45–54). Rotterdam, NL: Sense Publishers.

Davidson, D. J. (Ed.). (2003). *The wisdom of Theodore Roosevelt*. New York, NY: Citadel Press.

Darling-Hammond, L. (1999). *Teaching as the learning profession*. San Francisco, CA: Jossey-Bass.

DiCicco, T., & Hacker, C. (2002). *Catch them being good*. New York, NY: Penguin Group.

Donaldson, G. (2001). *Cultivating leadership in schools*. New York, NY: Teachers College Press.

Dormann, H. (1987). *The speaker's book of quotations*. New York, NY: Balantine Books.

Drucker, P. (1977). *People and performance: The best of Peter Drucker on management*. New York, NY: Routledge.

Elmore, R. (2005). *School reform from the inside out*. Cambridge, MA: Harvard Education Press.

Frontiera, J. (2006). The relationship between leadership, efficacy, belief, and performance among boys' high school basketball players (Master Thesis, West Virginia University).

Fullan, M. (2002, May). The change. *Educational Leadership*, 16.

Fullan, M. (2004). *Leading in a culture of change*. San Francisco, CA: Jossey-Bass.

Ginott, H. G. (1972). *Teacher and child*. New York, NY: Avon Books.

Glasser, W. (1990). *The quality school*. New York, NY: Harper Collins.

Goleman, D. (1995). *Emotional intelligence*. New York, NY: Bantam Books.

Hagstrom, D. (2004). *From outrageous to inspired*. San Francisco, CA: Jossey-Bass.

Heider, J. (1985). *The Tao of leadership: Leadership strategies for a new age*. Atlanta, GA: Humanics Limited.

Heifetz, R. (1994). *Leadership without easy answers*. Boston, MA: President and Fellows of Harvard College.

Heilbrun, C. G. (1988). *Writing a woman's life*. New York, NY: Norton.

Jackson, P. (1995). *Sacred hoops*. New York, NY: Hyperion.

Kenow, L., & Williams, J. (1999, June). Coach-athlete compatibility and athlete's perception of coaching behaviors. *Journal of Sport Behavior, 22*(2), 251.

Kohn, A. (1999). *The schools our children deserve*. New York, NY: Houghton Mifflin.

Kramp, M. K. (2004). Exploring life and experience through narrative inquiry. In K. de Marris & S. D. Lapan (Eds.), *Foundations for research: Methods of inquiry in education and the social sciences* (pp. 103–122). Mahwah, NJ: Lawrence Erlbaum Associates.

Kramer, J. (1970). *Lombardi: Winning is the only thing*. New York, NY: World Publishing.

Krzyzewski, M. (2000). *Leading with the heart*. New York, NY: Warner Books.

Larson, J. (1955, February). Athletics and good citizenship. *Journal of Educational Sociology, 28*(6), 257–259.

Longenecker, C., & Pinkel, G. (1997, February). Coaching to win at work. *Manage, 48*(2), 19–24.

Marshall, S. (2006). *The power to transform*. SanFrancisco, CA: Jossey-Bass.

Marzano, R., & Pickering, D. (2011). *The highly engaged classroom*. Bloomington, IN: Marzano Research Laboratory.

Meier, D. (1995). *The Power of their ideas*. Boston, MA: Beacon Press.

Moskal, B. (1997, October 6). Coaching a turnaround. *Industry Week/IW, 246*(18), 48–54.

Patton, M. Q. (2002). *Qualitative research and evaluation methods* (3rd ed.). Newbury Park, CA: Sage Publications.

Pink, D. (2005). *A whole new mind*. New York, NY: Penguin Group.

Phillips, D. (1992). *Lincoln on leadership*. New York, NY: Warner Books.

Pressfield, S. (2005). *Gates of fire*. New York, NY: Bantam.

Reeves, D. (2002). *The daily disciplines of leadership*. San Francisco, CA: Jossey-Bass.

Riley, P. (1993). *The winner within.* New York, NY: Berkley.

Robertson, D. (2003, May). So you want to be a leader? *Manage Online, 1*(4), N.PAG-N.PAG. Retrieved July 26, 2007, from Business Source Complete database.

Robinson, K. (2009). *The element.* New York, NY: Penguin Group.

Schlechty, P. (2011). Engaging students. San Francisco, CA: Jossey-Bass.

Senge, P. (1990). *The fifth discipline.* New York, NY: Doubleday/ Currency.

Sergiovanni, T. (1982, February). Ten principles of quality leadership. *Educational Leadership,* 330.

Sergiovanni, T. (1984, February). Leadership and excellence in schooling. *Educational Leadership,* 4.

Sergiovanni, T. (1995a, May 10). Schools are special places. *Education Week, 14*(33), 48.

Sergiovanni, T. (1995b, Fall). The principal as staff developer. *Journal of Staff Development, 16*(4), 1–5.

Sergiovanni, T. (1995c). *The principalship: A reflective practice perspective.* Needham Heights, MA: Allyn and Bacon.

Sergiovanni, T. (2004, May). Building a community of hope. *Educational Leadership,* 33.

Sizer, T. (1996). *Horace's hope.* New York, NY: Houghton Mifflin.

Smith, J., Carson, K., & Alexander, R. (1984, December). Leadership: It can make a difference. *The Academy of Management Journal, 27*(4), 765–767.

Smoll, F. & Smith, R. (1989). Leadership behaviors in sport. Journal of Applied Social Psychology, 19, 1522-1551.

Spradley, J. (1979). *The ethnographic interview.* Fort Worth, TX: Harcourt Brace.

Terkel, S. (1972). *Working.* New York, NY: Pantheon.

Thoreau, H. (1971). *Walden.* Princeton, NJ: Princeton University Press.

Tough, P. (2012). *How children succeed: Grit, curiosity, and the hidden power of character.* New York, NY: Houghton Mifflin Harcourt.

Tyler, R. (1949). *Basic principles of curriculum and instruction.* Chicago, IL: Chicago Press.

Unsworth, T. (1997, January 24). Chicago Bulls head pastor, Phil Jackson. *National Catholic Reporter, 33*(12), 29–31.

Wagner, T. (2003). *Making the grade.* New York, NY: RoutledgeFalmer.

Wagner, T. (2012). *Creating innovators.* New York, NY: Scribner.

Wall, B. (2007, January). Being smart only takes you so far. *Training & Development,* 64.

Westering, F. (2006). *Make the big time where you are.* New York, NY: McGraw Hill.

Wheatley, M. (1992). *Leadership and the new science.* San Francisco, CA: Berrett-Koehler.

Wood, G. H. (1998). *A time to learn.* New York, NY: Penguin Group.

Wooden, J. (1999). *Practical modern basketball.* Needham Heights, MA: Allyn and Bacon.

Zhao, Y. (2009). *Catching up or leading the way.* Alexandria, VA: ASCD.

Zinn, D. (2000, February). General Colin Powell's 13 rules on leadership. *Coach & Athletic Director, 69*(7), 52.

APPENDIX A

CHICAGO THREE INTERVIEW QUESTIONS

1. Why basketball?

2. What inspires you?

3. Why are you valuable?

4. I'm really good at...

5. I am inadequate in...

6. Why are you valuable to your school?

7. Describe a time(s) or experience that defined your life/career.

8. Share what you have learned from other leaders/coaches.

9. Define your philosophy.

10. Do you have doubts?

11. How has your family past and present shaped your philosophy?

12. Provide examples of personal failure and your responses.

13. Why have you flourished in a profession that destroys so many?

14. Share your GOLD. Secret recipes.

15. How have you evolved?

16. One sentence advice for young leaders/teachers/coaches.